A School of the Lord's Service

Therefore we must establish a school
of the Lord's service, in founding
which we hope to ordain nothing
which is harsh or burdensome.

Rule of St Benedict, Prologue

A School of the Lord's Service

A HISTORY OF

AMPLEFORTH

Anthony Marett-Crosby OSB

Designed by Robin Farrow

Originated, printed and bound by Butler & Tanner, Frome, Somerset

Published by James & James (Publishers) Ltd.

Illustrations
Title page: Sunday Mass
Below: Looking south from Central Building.

Foreword

Two hundred years in the landscape of the Ampleforth Valley is not long; churches and houses in the villages of Ampleforth, Gilling East and Oswaldkirk are much older and so too is the castle standing prominently above Gilling. But one section on the north side of that valley has been much altered in those years, the site where Fr Bolton's retirement home was built from 1783.

This is the story of that site. Fr Bolton's house has now gone and been replaced by a range of buildings dominated by the Abbey Church. This is the Ampleforth campus, home of the Ampleforth Community of Benedictine monks and a centre for thousands of lay men and women, living nearby or far away.

This is a story not just of human endeavour, though there has been plenty of it from monks and lay people alike, nor is it just the story of dedicated and generous support of money and skill, without which nothing much would have been achieved, but, most important of all, it is the story of God's guiding hand leading the remnants of a monastic community to this place, enabling it to put down roots and inspiring its Benedictine spirit to spread outwards. It has all happened since 1802.

At the centre of every family of monks is the call from God. That call, however expressed, and it is different for each monk, is expressed in a life of prayer, community living and hard work, the central elements of a monk's life. This community of monks from its inheritance from that at Westminster Abbey, London, through its years of exile in France, and now celebrating its bicentenary at Ampleforth, has always put a high priority on work in school, parish or hospitality. In this way our 'family spirit' has developed, characterised by realism, a sense of humour, and a desire to help wherever we can.

Our Bicentenary celebration is shared with our wider family, both here at Ampleforth and in places throughout Britain and overseas. To every one in this family we owe so much, whether expressed in their daily work to keep us healthy and cheerful, or by their generous support and loyalty as former members of staff, Old Boys, visitors or friends. This book is a sign of our gratitude. We acknowledge their patience with our eccentricities and their understanding with our mistakes. During this year we pray especially for them.

Finally, this book is an act of gratitude to the gifts that God has given us. Through it we renew our dedication to God, our only guarantee for the future.

Timothy Wright OSB, Abbot

Preface

This book has come together through the collaboration of many members of the Ample-forth Community and its friends. I am grateful to all of those who have given so freely of their memories, and who have brought alive for me the history of the Community, parishes and schools in the twentieth century. Many old Amplefordians committed these memories to writing, and these have formed an invaluable source of history, legend and detail.

I would like to express my profound thanks to Fr Abbot for his Foreword, to Fr Leo, to Sir David Goodall for their chapters, to Peter Galliver, Fr Adrian, Fr Dominic and Fr Henry for their sections, and further advice, comment and stories which have been most valuable. Without them, this work would have been immeasurably the poorer. I would also like to thank all those members of the Community who have contributed reminiscences and character sketches for inclusion. Sadly, it was not possible to include all of these in the final text.

I would like to acknowledge in a special way the help and encouragement that I have received from Fr Anselm. His own immense knowledge of the history of the Community has been a constant resource, always available at the end of the telephone. His help in the selection of archival photographs has also been essential to the putting together of this work.

None of this would have been possible without the help of Susie Green, who with unfailing care and good humour transcribed the text, collated the text boxes and captions, and put up with the many corrections and changes of mind which have afflicted her. Her patience and support, along with that of Jan and Yvonne in the Pastoral Office, has made this book possible.

Throughout the preparatory period, I have been given assistance in all sorts of ways by Hamish MacGibbon and the staff of James & James. I would like to express my gratitude for their enthusiasm and support.

Just a few days before he died in his eighty-sixth year, Fr Vincent Wace sat with me for two hours in the sun, reminiscing about his days as a boy in the Junior House. Those memories, entirely accurate at every point where I could check them, were matched only by his enthusiasm for the project as a whole. If this book has a dedication, it is to him and to all members of the Community who have gone before us and who watch over us still.

Anthony Marett-Crosby OSB
August 2001

Contents

Arrivals

It has never been easy to get to Ampleforth. The journey is frequently beautiful, sometimes breathtaking, but rarely quick. It seems it has always been so. For the first half of the 19th century, the only available public transport was the coach and horses that travelled between York and Helmsley three times a week. This came no closer to Ampleforth than the Oswald-kirk road, so the last stage of the journey was very frequently done on foot. Sometimes, and especially in bad weather, boys and monks alike could be met by a cart pulled by the college donkey, Neddy. This legendary beast was an important member of the Community at Ampleforth, living in a small paddock adjacent to the original chapel of the Old House. Inevitably, it strayed into this chapel from time to time, on one occasion interrupting a High Mass by wandering on to the sanctuary.

For visitors, getting out to Ampleforth could represent a considerable undertaking. When the distinguished Professor of Memory, Dr Feinaigle, first came to teach at Ampleforth, the length of the journey required him to spend a night at the Station Hotel in York. The following morning, he caught the coach to Oswaldkirk, and had just settled in his seat when one of the hotel boys was seen to be running after the departing vehicle: He shouted at the coachman: 'Stop, stop! The memory man has forgotten his umbrella!' The coaches themselves, and especially Ampleforth's own carts, were not remembered for their comfort. When the original college cart was replaced by a shandry, there was little improvement in appearance but apparently it provided a better journey, or at least held out 'the prospect of an occasional ride within the limit of hope, for at a crush it might hold six.' This vehicle was replaced first by a more aesthetically pleasing one and later by a four-wheeled carriage, the last of which offered, for the first time in the history of Ampleforth, the chance of a ride from Oswaldkirk to Ampleforth without getting wet.

The experience of arriving by horse-drawn transport endured well into the 20th century. One old Amplefordian remembers being met in April 1914 by the school wagonette, capable of conveying at least ten passengers even though it was drawn by a single horse. During the journey from Gilling station to the college, the coachman lost control, and the horse ran off down a hill, leaving the wagonette swaying perilously in its wake. Fortunately, the boy's uncle had more presence of mind, or willingness to take risks, than did the coachman, and

Facing page: Sir Giles Gilbert Scott's High Altar arch, completed 1920s.

1

so this visitor leapt out of the moving wagon to restrain the beast, which later was found to have gone wild because of a bee in its ear. All in all, it was a somewhat unexpected way to arrive, although the brave uncle was rewarded for his labours with a suitably refreshing drink. The young boy meanwhile, along with his brother, was entertained until the arrival of the rest of the school by Fr Sebastian Lambert, who tried without any success to show them how to play handball.

The availability of horse-drawn transport made possible on rare occasions what has now become commonplace, namely the fond farewell of mother and son on the doorstep of the boy's house. In 1918, an 8-year-old boy beginning his education at Ampleforth was accompanied all the way to Gilling station by his mother, where a pony and trap had been hired in advance to make the last stage of the journey. After the slow, up-hill climb the two of them arrived at the preparatory school, where within five minutes mother had handed over her son and had returned, by way of the same trap, to catch the up train back to York.

By the end of the 19th century, a train had been running through the valley for more than 40 years. Certainly the establishment of the railway in 1853 made a huge difference, although it did not solve every difficulty. The line itself ran from Pilmoor, on the main route between York and Edinburgh, through the valley as far as Gilling, where it split into two parts, with the northern line going to Helmsley and Pickering and the eastern straight to Malton. Many of the recollections of Ampleforth in the late 19th and early 20th centuries focus on arriving by train, and especially on the school specials which ran from King's Cross to Gilling until the Easter of 1964. The normal passenger service was also frequented by monks, masters and boys, and with its neat green engines and crimson carriages it must have been quite a sight. It was also cheap, especially for those connected with Ampleforth; because the Community had supported the line against a rival company which had planned a new route, special discounts known as 'College tickets' could be purchased. In 1870 Prior Bede Prest asked for a special station to be built at Ampleforth College Gate, where the current valley road crosses the line of the railway. This never came to pass, so generations of monks and boys disembarked at Gilling, with the longer trains having to pass through the station in two sections because the platform was too short. From Gilling, distinguished visitors were usually met by a wagon, but for many years the boys walked to school across the valley, except it seems in the event of snow. This remained true well into the 20th century. Fr Bernard Boyan remembered walking from the station to the Junior House in 1921, and it is said that a boy from overseas, burning with resentment at the prospect of this unexpected walk, threw his suitcase into the brook to express his frustration. How he was treated by the school authorities is not remembered, but his contemporaries regarded him as something of a hero.

The journey could be a happy occasion, more perhaps for old Amplefordians returning to visit than for the boys themselves, who vied to be in the end carriages because this prolonged the holidays by a few precious minutes. In 1893, a distinguished old boy returning for Exhibition recorded how:

> The time passed quickly enough in greetings and recognitions, in merry jests and reminiscences, in spite of the inevitable bore with the prodigious memory who, each time the train stopped, insisted on telling us the name of the next station. On we sped past the old White Horse – not very white now – past Coxwold church and Newburgh Priory and with just time for a glimpse of Byland among the hills and a glance at Fairfax among the trees . . . It was a gloomy grey afternoon, and we looked with some concern for the

2

Gilling Station. The School entrains, July 1962.

wagon to take our luggage. It was not visible, and instead there was Br John with one dog-cart to carry the impedimenta of some thirty guests. Of course, most of it had to be left in the wet grass.

For a time, Ampleforth also had its own private tramway, running from the sidings at Gilling along the line of the railway and then turning north across the valley. Its main purpose was to provide coal for the gasworks built in the early 1890s, but building materials and other goods were also brought up, mostly in horse drawn trucks until the arrival of an engine in the early 1920s. Sometimes the boys came this way too, travelling in the same trucks as were used for goods.

There were inevitable incidents involving this tramway. In 1909, the younger boys were delighted to watch a wagon run out of control down the line, crashing through a gate and coming to rest in a hay field, spreading coal over a wide area. On another occasion, some boys climbed into a wagon, which then ran too fast and tipped them into the brook. In fact, there was a small passenger wagon, but it was used very rarely and the line itself fell out of use with the coming of electricity, being formally abandoned by 1930. Even then, the tramway had its uses. It became a favourite run for winter tobogganing, with at least one person remembering a non-stop descent from Aumit Hill via the gasworks to the top cricket pitch.

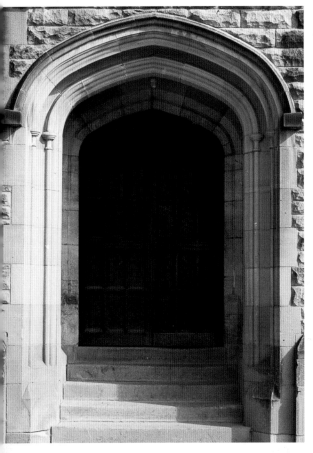

Memorial Doors, to those who died in the train fire, 28 April 1941.

The Royal Air Force biplane which crashed on take-off, c.1919.

After the Second World War, the railway line itself gradually declined, closing to normal passenger traffic in 1953 and finally being laid to rest in 1964. Only once, in 1941, did disaster overtake the school train. A fire started in one carriage as the school train was running north near Grantham, and six boys died in the blaze. The rest of the train continued its journey, but the railway fire has remained long in the memory of Ampleforth, and the names of the boys killed are inscribed on the Thompson doors at the south end of the big passage.

Long after its demise, the railway continued to exert an unlikely influence on monastic life – the timing of the Abbot's Council was, for some 20 years after the end of the railway, determined by the arrival of the last train that would have brought the parish fathers over from Lancashire.

For many years, the bus journey from York to Ampleforth has been a source of relaxation rather than speed. Writing in 1953, Fr George Forbes, a great lover of the railway, lamented:

> It is curious to reflect that one result of the withdrawal of the trains has been a general increase in the time required to travel . . . To reach Ampleforth in time for the evening meal it is necessary today to leave London one hour earlier than it was in 1910.

It is no surprise that some adventurous souls have sought more exciting means of transport. A legend relates that the first person to arrive at Ampleforth by air was an old boy, a member of the Royal Flying Corps, who in 1918 flew into the valley in a biplane. All went well until the take-off, when for reasons unknown it crashed on to the east side of the cricket field. The pilot was unhurt, but perhaps the pride of this new arm of the military service was dented, so the next day, two more biplanes were flown in to take the stranded pilot out. Unfortunately, when one of these replacement aircraft was landing, it collided with the railings that used to surround the cricket field, crashing and finishing up on its nose next to the tramway. The story has grown, but the crash was real. Perhaps the valley is on the whole more suited to helicopters than to aircraft, and occasional visitors, both military and civilian, have made use of this form of transport when all else seemed just too slow.

The arrival of the first car at Ampleforth bearing a boy for the school is recorded in a wonderful photograph. The date is September 1901, and it captures a mix of the eminently Victorian, especially the hats being displayed, and the apparently contemporary. The monastic habits have not changed at all, and the stone arch in the background is still where it has always been, half way down the main drive. In the front sits a proud father with his new toy, and the small boy in the back is the future Fr Stephen Marwood, clothed as a monk in 1907 and the first housemaster of St Oswald's from 1926 to 1949.

There have always been people who have come to Ampleforth by accident, a fact which sometimes displeases those who tend to imagine that the Abbey and College are located at the centre of the universe. Many summer afternoons are marked by the arrival of perplexed holidaymakers, who have not the slightest idea what they have come to, but have been drawn either by the sight of the church tower from Yearsley bank or in the vain hope that they are finding a quick way to Helmsley. The first thing that these visitors experience is bewilderment, though most go away interested and some even enlightened.

Among the more astonishing stories of unexpected arrivals concerns James Shepherd, who in 1836 had packed his trunk in expectation of going overseas to be educated at the monastery of St Edmund at Douai. He was spending the night before this journey in a Liverpool hotel when an unnamed monk of Ampleforth, a priest at Seel Street in the city, arrived and immediately pronounced the boy to be suffering from high fever. He took him straight upstairs, put him to bed and then explained to an understandably anxious mother why the young boy could not possibly be expected to make the arduous journey. His companion on this journey was to have been the Prior of Douai, who was not able to wait for him and so left Liverpool alone. A few days later, the Shepherds were persuaded to let their son go to Ampleforth instead, and by a not very curious coincidence, the same monk from Seel Street was available to take him.

The first car, a Renault, at Ampleforth bearing Fr Stephen Marwood as a schoolboy, September 1901.

5

St Peter's, Seel Street, Liverpool.

It proved a rewarding if perhaps underhand manoeuvre, for the young boy James joined the monastic community and was professed as Br Laurence.

The Story

Every person who arrives at Ampleforth comes to visit a different place. They might be monks arriving to join the Community, mission fathers returning after years on the parishes, boys and now girl students arriving at school, guests of those boys, school lecturers, people coming on retreat or tourists who have no idea what they have come to at all. Many histories are intermeshed in the one place, and it is still possible to spend many years here without much awareness of what is going in other parts of the establishment.

At its heart, of course, Ampleforth is a monastic community. In telling the story of any other part of Ampleforth, we must never lose sight of this. This means that our narrative must focus on people before places, and it cannot be contained within tidy geographical boundaries. The work of the Community has always extended beyond the confines of the valley, and to talk of Ampleforth without giving due weight to the missions, parishes and other foundations would be to distort the picture. So this is not simply a school history, nor the history of a religious order, nor even the history of a place. It is all of these things and more, because it is a celebration of the story of a community, which has been and remains many faceted, outward looking and also ever changing.

It is also a story that has been told before. The first history of Ampleforth was that written by Fr Cuthbert Almond to celebrate the first centenary of 1903, and this beautiful book remains an invaluable source of information and illustrations. Many of the line drawings in the pages that follow are drawn from the artistic work commissioned for Almond's volume, some by Joseph Pike and more by Fr Maurus Powell and Almond himself. Then in 1952 came a serious work of scholarship, *Ampleforth and its Origins*, edited by Abbot Justin McCann and Fr Columba Cary-Elwes. This work reflects the interests of the scholars within the Community at that time, and is especially notable for the remarkable chapters on the early history of the Community written by Abbot McCann and John Hugh Aveling. It also contains a poignant and powerful introduction to the monastic ideal as experienced at Ampleforth by Abbot Herbert Byrne.

More recent scholarship has augmented some but by no means all of the work done in 1952. The modern volumes of the *Ampleforth Journal* contain all sorts of insights and explorations, mainly written by members of the Community and others. The most recent scholarly history is Ampleforth: *The Story of St Laurence's Abbey and Community (2000)* by Fr Anselm Cramer.

All of these works have much in common, and all share a common debt to the invisible labours of the monks who, over the last 200 years, have preserved the memories of the Community. Pre-eminent in this regard is the work of Fr Athanasius Allanson, whose massive labours constitute a treasury of facts and personalities from the 17th to the mid-19th centuries. Born in 1804, Allanson took his solemn vows in 1821, before his seventeenth birthday. He proceeded to ordination, and within a few months was posted to the mission at Swinburne, where he was to remain as its priest for 48 years, until his death in 1876. Over this time, he researched a monumental work, including a *History of the English Benedictines* and an extraordinary collection of biographies of every English Benedictine from the revival until

1850. These two sources are invaluable, and although Allanson later wrote that he 'cannot but record my deep and heartfelt regret that it has ever been my misfortune to attempt to compile the dull and uninteresting *Biography of the Benedictines*,' it remains a fascinating read. He tells us of 'zealous missioners', the occasional 'wearisome Father', and even 'an irresponsible (ie independent) Abbot'. Allanson knew that it is the members of the Community who are its real history.

But Allanson's work is painted on a broader canvas than the Ampleforth Community alone. He was writing the history not of a house but of the English Benedictine Congregation, the collective identity of English monasticism first formed in the 13th century and renewed in 1619. In the difficult years of the 17th century it established a structure of governance which endured for over two hundred years. The primary concern of the monks in this period was missionary, so the Congregation was centralised around an elected President, his Council (the Regimen) and a Provincial for each of two provinces, North and South. At its peak was the General Chapter, the legislative body of the Congregation, composed of these officials, the Cathedral Priors and, rather as an afterthought, the heads of each individual monastery. Within this structure, the actual monasteries played little part, even after they were established in England. The structure was changed in 1899 to allow for the independence of the monasteries as abbeys, but the concept of the Congregation, the General Chapter and its President endures to this day.

Fr Athanasius Allanson, 1804–76. A 1946 pencil sketch by Hector Whistler, made from a very early photograph.

The Congregation originally consisted of three monasteries of monks, known by the names of their patron Saints as St Gregory's, St Laurence's and St Edmund's, and the monastery of nuns founded at Cambari under the patronage of Our Lady of Consolation. Since then other monasteries have been founded, both of men and women, bringing the total at the time of writing to 13 independent houses. The sense of membership of this Congregation was strong in the early centuries, especially for monks serving on the missions, who could spend most of their lives far away from the original monastery of their profession. Until the end of the 19th century, it is much more meaningful to talk of Laurentians or Gregorians than of monks belonging to a particular place, since they rarely returned to that place, and anyway the monasteries moved. Thus what follows is the story of the Community of St Laurence, now at Ampleforth.

Within the Congregation, certain individuals have traditionally been honoured with the title of Cathedral Prior or Titular Abbot. Both forms of title refer back to the English monastic congregation before the Reformation, and in the 17th century the idea that the titles of the priories should be preserved, in the expectation that the Catholics would get them back, led to the establishment of nine Cathedral Priors. These were not mere honorifics, since the Cathedral Priors made up the most significant group within the General Chapter. The idea of granting the titles of ancient abbeys to monks is much more recent, and the story of how this came about is told elsewhere. But the presence of multiple Abbots and Priors can seem confusing, as the titles can mean very different things. Not all Abbots referred to in the pages that follow had actual abbeys.

It is not the intention of this volume to tell the story in the historical detail that some might like. This is done better elsewhere. Rather, this Bicentenary seemed an opportunity to offer not only a history but a celebration, in which many, specialist and non-specialist alike, will hopefully find much. Let us now begin that story.

The Community of Saint Laurence *before 1802*

Where to begin?

Monks very often do not know where to start their histories. In one sense, the beginning of the story told by this book is 1802, when two disheartened groups of English Benedictine monks arrived at Ampleforth. In fact, monks had lived at Ampleforth before. The Community only chose the place because Fr Anselm Bolton, a monk of the Community of St Laurence, had been given a house, perched on the northern edge of the Fairfax estate of Gilling, as a reward for 30 years of service as chaplain and estate steward. Before Fr Anselm, other English Benedictine monks had served the Gilling chaplaincy – there may have been monks here from as early as 1645, and certainly there was a continuous presence from 1673.

The monastic past of the valley goes back still further. In the Middle Ages, the land that made up the Fairfax and eventually the Ampleforth estate was largely in the hands of religious orders, with Cistercians at Byland and Augustinian Canons at Newburgh. A medieval notebook compiled by a monk of Byland records how the medieval inhabitants of Ampleforth village looked to both Byland and Newburgh for spiritual and material help in time of need. In one picturesque story, we hear of a tailor named Snowball who, while walking across the valley from Gilling to Ampleforth, encountered a lost soul in the form of a raven. It may have appeared much like those birds that still haunt the valley at dusk, save that this one had sparks of fire shooting from its side. Snowball forced the spirit to flee as far as the Holbeck – the brook, as known to many – and he then ran to Byland to gain the kind of spiritual consolation needed to give rest both to the spirit and to himself. The instinct to seek the help of God from monasteries may be said to run deep in this part of the world.

The story of monasticism in England reaches back to the double tradition of Celtic and Roman Monasticism. A powerful symbol of the continuity over these many centuries, and indeed of the continuity that links today's English Benedictines with their medieval predecessors, is the great abbey of Westminster on the bank of the River Thames. Its foundation and expansion during the late Anglo-Saxon period is associated with the great figures of St Dunstan and St Edward the Confessor, and in the early years of the Norman Conquest it was

Facing page: *Byland Abbey, west front.*

The Abbey Arms, 1922, derived from those of the Medieval Abbots of Westminster.

Below: *a medieval tile from Westminster Abbey in the sanctuary wall at Ampleforth.*

Arms of the medieval Westminster Abbots.

given new impetus by one of the great abbots of that generation, Gilbert Crispin. Over the Middle Ages, Westminster underwent the same gentle cycles of reform and stagnation, greatness and decline, that is common to the history of all great monastic houses. At the Reformation, Westminster was dissolved along with the other great houses, and in 1539 its fate seemed sealed.

That Westminster's history was to be different was the result of geography and politics. It was the most royal of the Benedictine houses and was at the centre of national life, so when Queen Mary chose to re-establish a single Benedictine house in 1555, she chose the monastery of Westminster forming a community out of some of the shattered remnants of the medieval monasteries. Personal links brought this group together, and at its centre was one of the great characters of the period, its only abbot John Feckenham.

In the end the Community had a little opportunity to discover itself, since in November 1558 both Queen Mary and her great Cardinal, Reginald Pole, died. On 21 January 1559, the new Queen Elizabeth was crowned in Westminster Abbey, and she soon dissolved the few communities that had been briefly re-established, and the Community dispersed. Feckenham himself was sent to the Tower of London, and spent his remaining years either in prison or under house arrest at Wisbech. His fate is a last testament to the power of a monastic vision for England, a vision that seemed to have died.

From Old to New

That it did not die completely is a double achievement, one personal and the other canonical. The personal continuity between this last gasp of medieval monasticism and its new scion is provided by Sigebert Buckley, the last surviving monk of the restored Community of Westminster. The formal canonical continuity was provided by the Apostolic See, which in 1619 and again in 1634 decreed that the newly formed houses of English monks were in continuity with those that had existed before the opening of the chasm of the Reformation. The Papal Bull *Plantata* of this year remains the foundation charter of the English Benedictine Congregation.

At the Dissolution of the monasteries, some English monks went abroad to pursue their vocations in less threatened parts of Europe. Although their number was comparatively small, it established enough of a precedent for other men seeking the monastic life to follow in their footsteps. The most popular destination appears to have been either Spain or Padua, where they joined existing monastic communities.

In the first years of the 17th century, steps were taken by these exiles to contact Sigebert Buckley, regarded as the last survivor of the Benedictine monastic tradition of the Middle Ages. Two monks, Robert Sadler and Edward Maihew, found the aged Buckley in Norfolk, and although they were already clothed as monks of a different congregation, Buckley aggregated them into the English Congregation, on 21 November 1607, handing over a tradition across the wide gap carved by the English Reformation. The date is still preserved in the English Congregation as its *Dies Memorabilis*.

This continuity provided the new men of the 17th century with a justification for pursuing the work of bringing the Catholic faith back to England. That work had indeed already started – the first monk to return to England as a missionary, Fr Augustine Bradshaw, had landed in England in 1603. The claim to continuity established the legitimacy of this mission, which was understood as the natural and necessary continuation of that monastic mission to the English first started by Augustine a millennium earlier.

10

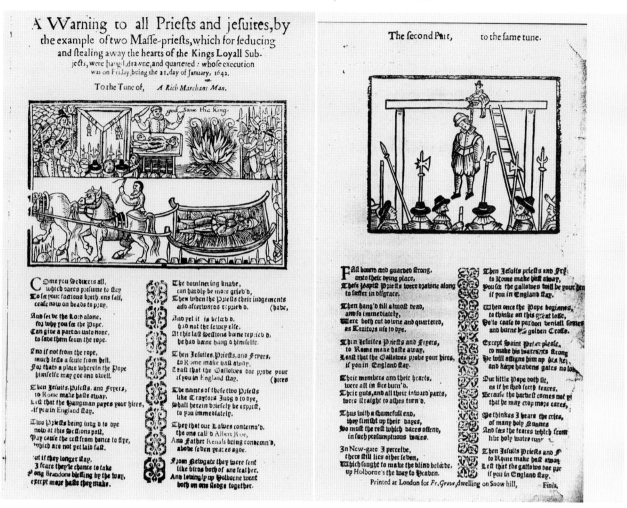

Popular broadsheet, 1642:
'A Warning to all Priests
and Jesuits'. Verse 11 names
'Albert Roe'.

The Missioners

Augustine Bradshaw was very much a representative of the new spirit of English monasticism. The mission to the English recusants meant working from the houses of the Catholic gentry, those few scattered families who remained loyal to the Church amidst the persecutions of the 16th and 17th centuries. Almost all such missionary monks lived alone, and did not run parishes in the modern sense. Some of the Catholic families did indeed have Catholic retainers and friends who were served by the missionary priests, but any public priestly work carried with it the huge risk of denunciation, arrest, trial and death. This martyrdom, shared by many secular priests, Jesuits and others serving the English Mission, did not pass by the Benedictine monks of the period.

Before turning to one such monk martyr, it is worth gaining some sense of the kind of monastic life lived by these missioners. Once in England, the monk remained a member of his monastic community, but in practice the missioners were subject to the authority of the Congregation. It was the President and the Provincials to whom the monks of this period

11

The altar front at Dieulouard – the Washing of the Feet.

looked for their appointments, and elevation to either office brought a good deal of practical authority over the missionary monks. The superiors of the particular houses exercised no authority beyond the walls of their own monastery, and had no claim over missioners who had been professed there. This created a highly centralised form of Benedictine life, unusual but not unknown in Benedictine history, a response to the emergency situation of missionary work in a hostile land.

Within this, the individual monk missioner had inevitably a great deal of autonomy. It was his responsibility to respond to the particular circumstances of the Mission, acting more or less in secret as the political conditions required. Many monks spent their whole active lives serving a single Mission supported by their own personal finances. Their biographies reveal individuals with strong personalities, working in circumstances of huge personal risk, fired by zeal for the faith and by the example of those called to pay the ultimate sacrifice.

Saint Alban Roe

While there were many missioners who served without attracting too much hostile attention, those who suffered imprisonment and martyrdom have become the icons of this age of Catholic endeavour. Amongst the canonised martyrs of England and Wales in this period is counted St Alban Roe, a monk of St Laurence at Dieulouard, who was executed at Tyburn on 21 January 1642. His life and death demonstrate much of the inner spirit of the missionary monks.

Bartholomew Roe was born a Protestant, and he converted after encountering a Catholic imprisoned in St Albans Abbey gaol. In 1608 he entered the English College at Douai, one of the most important seminaries for the training of secular priests for the English Mission. Three years later, Roe was expelled for insubordination, but two years after this he entered Dieulouard. The record of his expulsion from Douai makes serious reading – his superiors wrote, 'We consider him not at all fitted for the purposes of this college, on account of his contempt for the discipline'.

A contemorary drawing of Dieulouard just before the French Revolution (the size exaggerated – there were only two stories).

How this trait of character appealed to his monastic superiors, we do not know. He was ordained a priest at Dieulouard just two years after joining, and then sent on the English Mission. His secret work as a priest in London lasted just three years. In 1618 he was captured and imprisoned until pressure applied by the Spanish Ambassador secured his release in 1623, upon which he was banished from England on pain of death. Just a few months later, he returned to England, but again it was just three years before he was arrested, beginning a period of imprisonment lasting 16 years.

Ironically, this seems to have been the greatest period for his own mission. He used the Fleet prison as the base for his work of preaching and conversion, and was particularly remembered for his teaching on the practice of mental prayer. These tasks were achieved amidst continued and serious illness, but it seems to have been humour that saw him through. Indeed, some of those who knew him disapproved of the freedom with which he lived, particularly disliking his habits of gambling and drinking. His name is found amongst a list of undesirable persons prepared not by his Protestant captors but by a Catholic. Finally, in 1642, he was brought to trial, where he made little effort to defend himself. It is recorded that he told his judges that 'my Saviour has suffered far more for me than all that, and I am willing to suffer the worst of torments for his sake'.

On the feast of St Agnes, he and the 80-year-old Fr Thomas Reynolds were taken to their deaths. Reynolds is remembered as saying that 'I am glad that I have for my companion in death a person of your undaunted courage'. The account of his martyrdom suggests that humour, joy and bravery stayed with him to the end. In modern statues, he is sometimes shown holding a playing card in his right hand, a paradoxical symbol of a monk martyr but a sign, in its own way, of the sense of joy that permeates his story. His life and death reveal much of what was strongest in the monks of the age of persecution.

Dieulouard town coat of arms.

Dieulouard

The missionary imperative dominated the history of 17th and 18th century English monks, and it still exercises a profound influence over the self-understanding of their successors. At any one time, the overwhelming majority of the Community of St Laurence were far away from their monastic home.

Dieulouard today; part of the monastery, left.

This home was at Dieulouard, a small town now in eastern France. In the 17th century, it lay within the sphere of influence of the Duke of Lorraine, and in 1606 the Duke offered the English Benedictine monks a deserted collegiate church in the town. On 9 August 1608, the

A lasting consequence of the foundation of Dieulouard was the adoption of Roman martyr, St Laurence, as patron for the community.

Ampleforth coat-of-arms superimposed on a grid iron, emblem of the saint's martrydom, on the back of a Thompsons' 'Monk's Chair'.

fledgling community of Englishmen arrived, and found the abandoned buildings in so bad a state that they had to be rebuilt almost completely. Here they created a monastic home which lasted nearly 200 years.

It is difficult now to recover the feel of the 17th and 18th century life of Dieulouard. As a community, it was dominated by the demands of the English mission, and the Community must inevitably have been weighted towards those in training, although some senior monks always remained there and a very few retired there after years on the mission. There were also a handful of Frenchmen among them, lay brothers who served the immediate needs of the Community.

The history of Dieulouard was also shaped by its poverty. The size of the Community was determined by the extent of available income from rents and other business, and when the Community grew too large, new foundations had to be made, for example at St Malo in 1611. The monastery was also exposed to war, and during the Thirty Years War two of the Community were killed by passing Saxon troops on their way back from a sick call. Fire also destroyed parts of the monastery during the 18th century including its library. Its main source of income, apart from land, was the brewing of beer, and this, together with income from the small school, kept the monastery alive.

One of the most lasting consequences of the foundation of Dieulouard was the adoption of St Laurence as a patron for the Community. The abandoned Church was already dedicated to this Roman martyr, and the monks simply took over this saint with the site. It has often been said since that St Laurence found the Community rather than vice versa.

We know very little about the small school which was run by the Community at Dieulouard. There were probably about a dozen boys there at any one time, most of whom were destined for the priesthood and religious life. The small community of boys at Dieulouard existed alongside the monks, 'part cosy, part oppressive' in the words of John Hugh Aveling, in large measure as a stage on the path to monastic life.

The Return of the Exiles

The end of Dieulouard came swiftly, amidst the tumult of the French Revolution. The politics of the period caused alarm to the English monks in Lorraine from an early date, and in 1791 plans started to be made to pursue monastic life more secretly in the face of the new forces unleashed in France. In September 1793, a decree was issued that all foreigners resident in France would be imprisoned unless they carried special certificates of exemption, and although some passports were obtained, not all the Community was able to leave. Some were able to escape to Trier, but four monks and the lay brothers remained until October 12th.

The story of the escape of these last few monks of Dieulouard is one of the moments of high adventure in the history of the Community of St Laurence. The story focuses around the Prior, Richard Marsh, who later wrote up the story of his dramatic escape. His many adventures brought him in the end to England, where he gathered together the shattered remnants of his tiny flock. Dieulouard was lost, and though during the peace of Amiens some attempt was made to recover some of the possessions, the house the Community had was lost forever.

The return to England might have seemed a glorious homecoming; in fact there was nowhere to go. Although most of the Community was already in England, they were engaged in missionary work, and the establishment of a monastery would have aroused controversy and even conflict in many places. After a brief period at Acton Burnell, under the same roof as the monks of St Gregory's (later to go to Downside), and a short stay at a house in Birkenhead, the Community tried to settle at Brindle in Lancashire. The opposition of the local community, led very probably by the monk missioner there, saw off this attempt at a foundation. The very few monks left then moved to Scholes, Hall and Parbold. Then when scarlet fever overtook the small school that had been started at Vernon Hall, before it could move to more suitable accommodation, it seemed as if the history of this particular Community was approaching a sad end.

Vernon Hall, Liverpool.

This was certainly what Prior Marsh foresaw. At the General Chapter of 1802, he asked to be relieved of his leadership of the resident community, now just three priests and a single brother, and the Chapter turned to Fr Anselm Appleton to take over this remnant in his stead. It was he who led the Community to Ampleforth, although the mind behind the solution belonged to the President of the Congregation, Bede Brewer. Amongst the many other tasks he faced amidst the vicissitudes of war, he alighted on the solution for the Community of St Laurence, Fr Bolton's Ampleforth Lodge.

Left: *The 'hidden' church at Brindle, Lancashire.*

Brindle presbytery

15

3

Establishing Ampleforth
1802-62

Foundation

The history of the Community of St Laurence had not reached any obvious golden dawn in 1802. The arrival at Ampleforth Lodge was a clever solution to the problem of what to do with the remnant of the monks of Dieulouard, but there was no particular reason to believe that this move would be permanent, save that this time the monks owned the freehold of their home.

One difficulty faced by the Community was that the number of monks forming the resident community was tiny. Of those who had escaped from Dieulouard, some had moved on to the Mission, including Richard Marsh, so Fr Anselm Appleton came from the Mission at Knaresborough to become first Prior of Ampleforth. It seems that it was an unhappy choice. He was remembered as:

> a strict religious man, but his rough ways combined with a sour temper were not suited to give satisfaction to others and his Community gladly embraced the opportunity of superceding him at the next Chapter.

Richard Marsh, as President, 1837.

The man whose character and decisions were to shape the fledging community more than anyone else was President Bede Brewer. A monk of Saint Laurence's professed at Dieulouard, he had become a missioner at Bath and then at Woolton until he was suddenly made President by the death of Gregory Cowley. His first success had been his handling of the famously truculent Abbot Maurus Heatley of Lamspringe, and then he achieved the settlement of his Community at Ampleforth Lodge. Thereafter, he acted as the most powerful influence on a succession of early Priors. Only Richard Marsh, re-elected Prior in 1806, was sufficiently well established within the Community and the Congregation to make his own mark. Marsh was reluctant to accept the job, describing it as 'that very unpleasant office'. Marsh lived in the monastery over which he ruled for just a year after his appointment in 1806, after which he took on the mission at Aberford and divided his time between the two places.

16

When Fr Laurence Burgess was elected Prior in 1818, Brewer took up residence at Ampleforth, ensuring that he firmly implanted his ideals upon the way of life being established by the new Community. Brewer's influence was a threefold one. In the first place, he was able to pay for the necessary additions to Fr Bolton's house. Secondly, he was very influential in establishing the regime for the monks. He enjoined the monks to rise at 4 a.m. in the summer and at 5 a.m. in the winter, to observe specific periods of meditation and public devotional reading, and above all to maintain silence at meals and especially at breakfast. Brewer's influence probably led to the adoption of a form of habit worn by the resident monks, comprising a biretta, scapular and tunic. Thirdly, he undoubtedly played a part in the development of the school and its educational methods.

The Beginning of the School

The beginning of the school at Ampleforth is clear enough, but the early years are not otherwise well documented. General Chapter of 1802 told Parbold school to close, and said the 'Church Students' (possible monks) were to move to Ampleforth. In the event, many Parbold boys (including the future Earl of Shrewsbury) transferred to Stonyhurst, and Brewer organized the transfer to Ampleforth of the monastic school at Lamspringe in Germany, already in existence by 1671. This was suppressed by order of the Prussian Government in January 1803, the monks pensioned off, and the boys sent back to England. However, the

The Old House, c.1802 (artist unknown).

17

The Old House, c.1943, with left, the Chapel Wing, constructed c.1810.

King of Prussia agreed that the North Sea was not pleasant in winter, and undertook to pay for their keep till Easter. Their arrival at Hull on Easter Thursday, 14 April 1803, is recorded in one of Brewer's letters. By this time the school consisted of only twelve boys, but they included a future President (Molyneux) and Bishop (Baines). None of the Parbold names appears in the somewhat uncertain Ampleforth lists, which were written much later. Perhaps much of the early success of the education now offered at Ampleforth was derived from traditions, or abilities, brought over from Germany.

It is indeed clear that the early years of the school, which quickly became known as Ampleforth College, were highly successful. The charismatic personality of Fr Augustine Baines had much to do with this, but the school benefited also from the presence of Gregor Feinaigle, a former Cistercian monk employed at Ampleforth from about 1812 and famed for his teaching of memory techniques and his emphasis on public examinations. He and Baines seem to have been the driving forces behind a very forward-looking school. It is probably no accident that the earliest surviving Exhibition programme dates from two years after his arrival, and we know that Exhibition was held every year from 1814. This was also a period of building, most notably the construction in 1825 of the east wing of the Old House which in later years became the link building between the Old House and the 'New College'.

We can gain a glimpse of life in these early years at Ampleforth from the diary of Robert Nihell, a boy in the school who recorded events at Ampleforth during the year 1816. It is a characteristic schoolboy diary, and the first impression it gives is that, however good the education, Nihell had little or no grasp of spelling. It is full of incidental references to life in the valley, some of which will be recognised by any generation of monks or boys. For two days in February, the only entry made in the diary is the laconic phrase 'very muddy', while in May he noted, 'I began to write my geometry over again. Very cold'.

The diary is most valuable for the witness it gives to the intimacy of a small community in which there were few differences between boys and monks. The religious activities of the monastic community and that of the boys were closely knit, and comments on the sermons by the brethren pepper the diary. On Tuesday 20th February, Nihell noted that 'the four novices were professed after Vespers', but it seems that the only difference this profession made in their relationship with the school was that they moved from one part of the common refectory to another.

Such a vision of the early school is easy to idealise. This was after all a community of no more than ten monks and 80 boys in 1829. Many of these boys were destined for the priestly or religious life, as was noted in the public subscription document for the building of the west wing which advertised that 'a college has been opened at Ampleforth near York, for the purpose of bringing up youth to a religious life and qualifying them for the discharge of the ministerial functions'. But there were always some boys whose careers were less certain, and the Laity's Directory of 1812 mentions that 'a limited number of young gentlemen not designed for that state would be admitted'. This small Community was nevertheless marked by a remarkable singleness of purpose, and perhaps by confidence in the future. Sadly, any such confidence was to be short lived.

The Crisis

The cataclysmic change of fortune which overtook the Community in 1829–30 reversed much of the achievements to date and threatened to undo any precarious hold on stability. If one man is blamed for this, it is usually Augustine Baines. In the demonology of Ampleforth he tends to occupy pride of place. But standing back, it is hard not to admire him – one of the driving forces behind the growth of Ampleforth College in the early years of the century, a fine teacher, a preacher of repute, and from the age of 36, Coadjutor Bishop of the Western District with right of succession.

The eastern extension of Old House, c.1825. Right, Brewer's Refectory Wing, 1818.

As he surveyed his diocese, which lacked many of the provisions for education found elsewhere, Baines had his vision for the future. He foresaw a diocese with a monastery at its centre, forming the nucleus for a seminary and whose apostolic work would be concerned largely with the pastoral care of the district. When he shared this idea with the monks of Ampleforth in 1823, there was interest and even enthusiasm, and the Prior at least was prepared to consider the possibility of an exchange of buildings between Ampleforth and Downside in order to effect it. Downside, which lay within Baines's area, rejected it out of hand, to which Baines responded by suspending the faculties of Downside monks to administer the sacraments outside the monastery. Then in 1827, Baines took his ideas to Rome, where the Benedictine Cardinal Capellari, the future Pope Gregory XVI, was impressed by the scheme and especially by the man. There was a real possibility in the winter of 1827 that Baines, aged 40, would become a Cardinal.

But Baines had not gone to Rome only to propose his vision for the future of the western district. He also raised something far more deadly, the spectre that the re-establishment of the monasteries of the Congregation in England after the French Revolution had been done without Papal authority and that therefore the vows of all those professed there were invalid. This was a massive threat to the integrity of the Congregation, and unsurprisingly it spurred its leading men into action. President Augustine Birdsall sent a delegation to Rome to plead their cause, consisting of Richard Marsh and a monk of Downside, Joseph Brown. The mission started badly, with Capellari questioning whether their journey had even been necessary, but Marsh hints that early on they secured the favour of Capellari's right-hand man and fellow monastic Cardinal, Placid Zurla. Then Capellari heard of Brown's habit of keeping off the winter chill of Rome by skipping; he came to see this, was delighted, and Marsh and Brown found that doors previously closed to them were now open. Once they had gained an entry, they produced documents showing the validity of the foundations, and in 1830 Rome issued a rescript that, with characteristic Vatican skill, put to right anything in the validity of the professions that ever might have been wrong.

This was not the outcome which Baines had sought. He had not been inactive during the period, and in December 1829 he had bought Prior Park as the base for his new venture. But the tide was starting to turn against him and by the spring of 1830 three monks were ready to follow him from Ampleforth to Prior Park: the Prior, Laurence Burgess, the Procurator, Placid Metcalfe, and the sub-Prior, Cuthbert Rooker. On May 13th 1830 these three left to be joined later by a single Missioner, and they took with them three of the four novices, a quarter of the school and the herd of cows.

We cannot read the story of Baines only from the perspective of Ampleforth. There was no malice or intention to destroy the Community, and he and the others believed that what they were doing was right. But their departure had a huge effect on those who remained. Perhaps the saddest part of this story is that the disaster for Ampleforth soon became a disaster for Baines as well. Prior Park did enable many of his ideas for education to bear fruit, but in 1836 fire gutted the central building, saddling him with a burdensome debt. The seminary never

19

flourished, and wider plans that he conceived for a Catholic university never got off the ground. When this far-sighted man died in 1843, there was little left of his vision.

Bumping along the bottom

We gain a telling insight into the state of Ampleforth after the departure of Baines and his supporters from the pen of Benedict Glover, a missioner brought in at short notice to fill the gap. Glover's responsibilities lasted just months, but the chaos was such that he could write to President Augustine Birdsall after a few weeks at Ampleforth:

> It requires a stouter heart than I possess to bear up against such evils. There is nothing now which I do not fear. Every step we take is an immense step deeper than the previous one. It would be a great relief to me to find that the Attorney General had convicted me of being a monk and banished me to Siberia.

The man eventually entrusted with the task of bringing Ampleforth back from the brink was Fr Adrian Towers, not a monk of our Community. Towers had been professed at Lamspringe, and was certainly a man of energy, later remembered for his willingness to engage in controversy with any who opposed the Catholic faith. He was a man who in other circumstances had inspired people – the hope of the General Chapter was undoubtedly that he would inspire again.

The problems he faced were vast. The monastery had lost its three senior officials and the school had lost some of its boys' staff. One monk was called back from the mission to help out and the President sent up two monks of Downside to assist, including the future archbishop Ullathorne. The parlous state of the finances could not be ignored, and it was to prove a near disaster that Towers had so little skill at managing money. In fact, it seems what little money he did have in 1830 had gone by 1832, leading to a series of claims against Laurence Burgess that he had been dishonest in his financial transactions during the last years of his own administration. This claim was not proved, but it is a sign of the desperate situation that the issue was raised at all.

When faced with these huge difficulties, it is no wonder that Towers faltered. Baines, on hearing of the name of the new Prior, wrote simply 'poor Dick'. The General Chapter had not been wrong in its initial vision of appointing a dynamic figure who might act as a bridge between the different factions within the Community, but after just two years there were those who were actively seeking his replacement. After four years in office, there was little doubt that Towers would be replaced. Some things had improved, and new members of the Community had been professed. But the substantive issues of finance had not been resolved, and in 1834 the Chapter opted for a man who was in almost every respect Towers' opposite.

Fr Bede Day was chosen above all because of his reputation for carefulness. His work on the missions had been marked by a spirit of economy, and even in his personal appearance he was neat to the point of fastidiousness. It was said that on the day he died, those who tended him noticed that there was an ink stain on one of his hands. This seemed uncharacteristic, until it was remembered that one of the monks who had been watching in his room had spent the time writing a letter. Summoned away for a moment, he had in his hurry spilt a few drops of ink on the table near the bed of the dying man. On his return, he found Bede Day out of his bed and trying to clean up the spilt ink. Yet the four years of his Priorship did little to alleviate any of

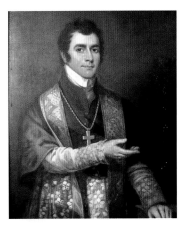

Bishop Augustine Baines.

Fr Adrian Towers, Prior 1830–34.

the fundamental problems that the Community faced, and in 1838 another change was called for. This third Prior proved to be the man who could turn the corner.

It would be good to know more about the school in these dark years. What evidence we have suggests that the school numbers held their own after the immediate debacle of the departure for Prior Park, but it is important to remember that, in this period, numbers in all Catholic schools were rising quickly. What is surely more important is that the guiding spirit of the school in its early years, Augustine Baines, had gone. He and others seem to have made the education at Ampleforth something very special, and it was this uniqueness which had perhaps disappeared.

Solid Foundations

The man who set change in motion was Anselm Cockshoot, Prior from 1838 to 1846. His early monastic career had been inevitably shaped by the Baines affair. He was clothed in 1822, and was resident at Ampleforth during the turbulent years leading up to the split in the Community. Indeed, Cockshoot was initially a supporter of the Baines scheme, and when the crisis erupted he was quickly sent away from Ampleforth to the mission at Coventry. There he spent eight years, and it seems to be this mission experience that marked him out as a future superior. His energy, application and achievement were all noted, and the school buildings he erected remained in service for some 40 years after him.

At the age of thirty-three Cockshoot was elected as Prior in succession to the weary and demoralised Bede Day. He faced the same grave burdens, but his manner of handling them was quite different to his predecessors. First of all he recognised his own weakness in financial affairs and so he sought the advice of those who knew about the handling of money. He arranged for three monks with sound financial brains – Alban Molyneux, Anselm Brewer and Athanasius Allanson – to be attached to the Council to provide financial advice, and their steadying hands had the desired effect. He was thus able to pay off the remaining debts, and even to invest money in the estate. Cockshoot embarked on a scheme for planting trees in the valley, and he even rebuilt the old inn at Byland, well known to later generations of monks and boys alike.

Within the monastery, Cockshoot achieved the renewed sense of confidence and industry that had eluded both Day and Towers. He made much of monastic studies, appointing a Professor of Theology for the monks and boys, and sending two of his brightest young monks, Austin Bury and Laurence Shepherd, to Parma to study theology. This was the first time any juniors had been sent away in this fashion, and although the 1848 Revolutions meant that they were unable to complete their studies in Italy, the effect on both men was considerable. Laurence Shepherd in particular seems to have used his time overseas to drink deeply from the sources of monastic theology that were feeding the new French monastery of Solesmes, ideas that he brought back and used later in life. It is possible that even after his eight years in office, it was not obvious to Cockshoot or anyone else that a corner had been turned. Later Priors built on his achievement, taking for granted both financial stability and the unity of the Community in the new endeavours that they undertook. In 1846, Cockshoot retired as Prior and went to the lonely mission of Holme-on-Spalding-Moor: later he had much influence on the founding of Belmont. Cockshoot's achievements came to fruition during the 13-year rule of Prior Wilfrid Cooper, probably the most ambitious superior that Ampleforth has ever had. He built on Cockshoot's foundations by an act of faith rather than by mere

Fr Laurence Burgess, as second Bishop of Clifton.

Wilfrid Cooper, Prior 1850–63.

*Ampleforth's first church.
Built by the brothers Joseph
and Charles Hansom,
1854–57, it replaced the
chapel in the Old House.
(photo c.1900)*

prudent management. Cooper created an Ampleforth not for his present but for a future he believed in.

Cooper's achievements are in the first place visible ones, and he more than any other 19th-century Prior is commemorated in buildings. First and most important, Cooper took the decision to build Ampleforth's first church, replacing the chapel in the old house which had served the Community since 1802. He approached the brothers Joseph and Charles Hansom, and after the purchase of property to the west of the old house, work started in 1854 and was finished in 1857.

The opening of the new church was the first occasion in the history of the Community's residence at Ampleforth when a truly grand event took place. It might have been the largest gathering of Benedictines in one place since the English Reformation. During the ceremony the choir sang the Nelson Mass by Joseph Haydn, then the Prior of Downside rose and preached a sermon on Saint Benedict to those who had assembled to witness this powerful statement of a monastic presence.

But Cooper's vision for the future required not only a new church but also a new college. Here, he was in part responding to real need, since Bolton's house was bursting at the seams. Again, Cooper turned to Joseph Hansom, who prepared two plans for an extension to the east of the old house. It is entirely characteristic of Cooper that he chose the grander version, and in 1859 building work began on the new site. A number of old buildings had to be demolished to make way for this, and it was not until 1861 that the new college was completed. To celebrate the event the boys had a whole week's holiday in the middle of the term, and the new stage at the southern end of the first floor of the new college was inaugurated with a performance of an original operetta written especially for the occasion.

Both the new church and the new college were bold statements of optimism and indicated considerable aspirations for the future. Both were larger than immediately necessary, and the new college in particular was designed to hold a school of a size in excess of the reality of 1861. Subsequent generations proved Cooper's vision right, but at the time his decision to build on such a scale was controversial. He had been restrained during the building of the church by the intervention of the President of the Congregation, Alban Molyneux, but the new college, estimated to cost £7,000, in fact cost £13,000. Cooper was criticised during the General Chapter for financial imprudence, that besetting difficulty for mid-century Priors, and he resigned in 1863.

This might seem a somewhat inglorious end to Cooper's time as Prior. There is no evidence that he felt it to be so; he returned to Liverpool and continued to work there until in 1875 he retired to the rural parish of Clayton Green near his birthplace at Brownedge. He died in 1877.

If Cooper's vision seems grand, it is important to remember the context in which it was effected. The 1850s were a period of remarkable optimism in English Roman Catholicism, beginning with the restoration of the hierarchy of Bishops in 1850. Cooper and his contemporaries believed in their mission, and they confidently expected the conversion of England. Ampleforth built its new church during a period of rapid, almost frenetic, building in Roman Catholic parishes up and down the country. That missionary need remained the principal work of the Ampleforth Community throughout these years – Cooper's Ampleforth was now ready to play its part in it.

4

The Nineteenth-Century College

There is only one history of 19th-century Ampleforth, just as there was only one name for the Community of monks and boys until 1898. The Community never styled itself 'Ampleforth Priory', and only adopted the title Abbey after the elevation of the monastery to that status. Before then, it was always and only Ampleforth College, a title retained in the postal address. It was practical to have one name, and also it was accurate – there was little clear distinction for much of the century between the life of the resident monks and the lifestyle of the boys in the school. Inevitably, the gradual extension of the school to the east by the building of the new college had an impact on this, such that monastery and school started to become at least geographically more distinct.

The Work of the College

Throughout the 19th century, the college occupied the energies of a significant number of monks. They tended to be the younger members of the Community, since frequently work with the boys ran alongside theological study or took place in the period immediately after ordination. Throughout the century, the Priors played a very considerable part in the day-to-day running of the school, as well as the broader setting of policy. It was under the name of the Prior that notices to parents were issued, and individual Priors could play a decisive role in the shaping of the education experienced by the boys. This is especially true of those Priors who had a natural interest in such matters, as did Anselm Burge.

From the perspective of the boys, however, the most visible figure in the daily life of the school was the First Prefect, a monk with general responsibility for discipline. We can sense something of his role in the school rules of 1822, which place all the responsibility for the boys with him. Here it becomes clear that Ampleforth was different from the great Anglican public schools of the period, for there is no mention of the delegation of authority to senior boys that was the custom elsewhere. Indeed, the early records of Ampleforth suggest that the First Prefect and his assistants were in close contact with the boys at all times.

This system seems to have worked. There is no evidence at Ampleforth of the kind of brutality sometimes ascribed to 19th-century public schools, and the system appears to have made

The first VI form, 1911. Standing, left, Noel Chamberlain, father of the present Headmaster.

corporal punishment an exception to the norm. The structure of discipline depended on tokens, which were given out to boys five minutes before the beginning of study every day. These tokens could be lost for the usual offences committed by students in any age, and for each loss of token there was a consequent loss of some part of recreation. Once boys had lost all their tokens, they began to collect extra work, which could often extend to the writing of Latin verse during a free evening. The First Prefect controlled this system, and he nominated a master to be responsible for the penance time when particular punishments were completed. Some of the penances listed are slightly surprising – it is noted that any boy going out of chapel during Mass 'must study a quarter of an hour during the penance time', and a similar punishment was distributed to those who woke up late, or who walked on the refectory tables during a meal.

For most of the first 60 years of its existence, the school was accommodated in Fr Bolton's original house. It is easy to be romantic about this, but the following extract from an undated letter of 1846 gives a more realistic picture of what it might have been like:

> Of course I have been under great apprehension for the safety of the 30 boys who sleep in the crazy building. I saw the absolute necessity of building up the sinking roof and falling wall with iron tie-rods, but I was afraid to do anything upon my own judgment alone. I therefore sent for Mr Hansom . . . About a month ago he examined the building and declared it in a most dangerous state. He said that he would not allow a child of his to sleep one night in it. I obtained from him a written formal opinion on the state of the edifice. He required the ironwork to be put up with as little delay as possible.

At the heart of the life of the school in the early period was the playroom, which until the building of the new College was in the eastern extension of the old house built on in the 1820s. At each end of the playroom were rows of drawers for the students, and beneath these

24

were the cupboards for shoes. The main body of the room was furnished sparsely, with two or three tables with seats attached to each side. The great feature was the stove in the centre, with a bench around it forming a circle known to the boys as 'the ring'. The room was without pictures or decoration, and the walls were unadorned apart, presumably, from the inevitable marks left by the boys' various activities.

Recollections of the playroom seem to focus on the stove, presumably because it was one of the few warm places in the building. Most boys tried to stand between the bench and the stove, because one could get nearer the heat, and these places were highly prized. Indeed, a custom existed whereby the area within the ring was packed full by the boys so as to prohibit anyone from breaking in, and forcing anyone who tried back out into in the cold.

There was little to do in the playroom. Certainly, in a room shared by boys of all ages, there would have been little opportunity to do anything quiet, and those who did want an understandable time of solitude had to request 'leave to the study' to go to read. When groups of boys did try to read in the playroom, they had to light a dip candle on one of the tables and then gather round it. It is remembered how other boys, seeing them at their reading, would try to throw their caps onto the dip candle and plunge the group into darkness.

To the east of this playroom was the washroom, a stone-flagged room of perhaps fifteen square feet. On three sides were stone troughs, with about a dozen taps spaced at intervals along it. In one corner was the cistern, and adjoining it a copper vessel for the supply of hot water on Saturday nights. Each boy had a basin, of tin or of wood, and each boy kept his towel, comb and other needs in his box in the playroom. Abbot Prest remarks of this room that it was 'adequate to necessity and absolutely free from the absolute suspicion of extravagance'. This is not hard to believe.

In this context, the building of the new college must have seemed like a new world. It was and remains a great building, a confident statement by Fr Cooper of where he wanted the

Prior Anselm Burge, 1885–97.

Memorial window to Prior Anselm Burge (North Aisle).

school to go. The new playrooms occupied the central part of what is now the school library, and above it was the splendid long room still known as the Big Study. This was a well-lit and cheerful space, furnished with desks and with a passageway through the centre. The presiding desk was in the oriel, as it has remained.

The boys and their studies

There is every reason to believe that in the early decades, the education at Ampleforth was of a remarkably high quality. The curriculum was certainly broad, as revealed in the prospectus of the examination of studies that took place in 1814. This was the forerunner of the modern Exhibition, during which boys described their studies in the three classical languages of Hebrew, Greek and Latin, and their work in French, history, geography, natural history, ornithology and botany. That this breadth of work represented a deliberate education policy is seen in a message to parents of 1815, in which school authorities wrote that:

> They feel confident that without any detriment to the classical part of education, a competitive knowledge of the most useful sciences can be communicated in the time that is usually given to languages alone.

The Big Study, looking south, c.1910.

The year 1815, indeed, saw something of a revolution in the course of studies, when it was decided that the boys would study French a year before they began Greek. This development needs to be seen in the context of the Anglican public schools of the period, where classicism was entirely in the ascendant. In 1817, Ampleforth spoke of its education in 'universal grammar', and aimed at establishing in the boys' 'close attention, cool abstraction and accurate reasoning'.

Two particular features of the education in these decades are worthy of note. In the first place, it seems that attention was given to natural history, which was an interest pursued throughout his life by the future Prior, Anselm Cockshoot. Secondly, scattered references suggest that a wide range of modern languages was taught, including Italian and Spanish in 1817, and Arabic in 1820.

All of these subjects were examined by monthly tests. During the Tuesday and Wednesday of the first week of each month, masters were required to set exams. A series of notes prepared by a first prefect adds that 'each professor and master is to state in writing . . . what their respective classes have learnt'.

The guiding hand behind this system of education was Augustine Baines. He engaged the services of Dr Feinaigle, and between them they created a structure of learning that was deliberately different from that available in other schools. Writing in 1817, parents were told that the school authorities:

> Ask for no premature verdict in favour of their system of education. It has hitherto been impeded in its progress by many disadvantages, naturally incident to the recent establishment of the school itself, and still more to the adoption of a new method of study. Notwithstanding all these disadvantages, the conductors of the studies look back with great satisfaction to what has already been done, and confidently appeal to the general result of the last two examinations. Hence forward, the students will enter on, and pursue their career under much better auspices.

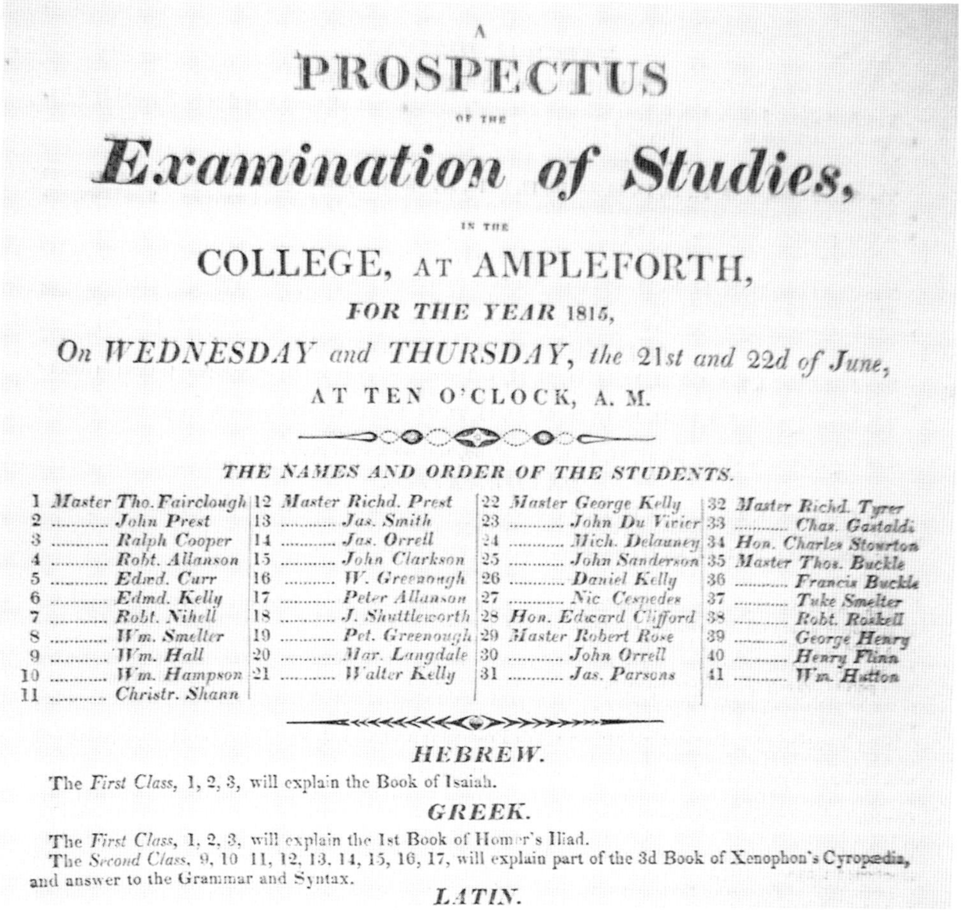

Exhibition progamme, 1815.

A

PROSPECTUS

OF THE

Examination of Studies,

IN THE

COLLEGE, AT AMPLEFORTH,

FOR THE YEAR 1815,

On WEDNESDAY and THURSDAY, the 21st and 22d of June,

AT TEN O'CLOCK, A. M.

THE NAMES AND ORDER OF THE STUDENTS.

1	Master Tho. Fairclough	12	Master Richd. Prest	22	Master George Kelly	32	Master Richd. Tyrer
2	John Prest	13	Jas. Smith	23	John Du Virier	33	Chas. Gastaldi
3	Ralph Cooper	14	Jas. Orrell	24	Mich. Delauney	34	Hon. Charles Stourton
4	Robt. Allanson	15	John Clarkson	25	John Sanderson	35	Master Thos. Buckle
5	Edmd. Carr	16	W. Greenough	26	Daniel Kelly	36	Francis Buckle
6	Edmd. Kelly	17	Peter Allanson	27	Nic Cespedes	37	Tuke Smelter
7	Robt. Nihell	18	J. Shuttleworth	28	Hon. Edward Clifford	38	Robt. Roskell
8	Wm. Smelter	19	Pet. Greenough	29	Master Robert Rose	39	George Henry
9	Wm. Hall	20	Mar. Langdale	30	John Orrell	40	Henry Flinn
10	Wm. Hampson	21	Walter Kelly	31	Jas. Parsons	41	Wm. Hutton
11	Christr. Shann						

HEBREW.

The *First Class*, 1, 2, 3, will explain the Book of Isaiah.

GREEK.

The *First Class*, 1, 2, 3, will explain the 1st Book of Homer's Iliad.

The *Second Class*, 9, 10 11, 12, 13, 14, 15, 16, 17, will explain part of the 3d Book of Xenophon's Cyropædia, and answer to the Grammar and Syntax.

LATIN.

The very novelty of this system made the departure of Baines all the more massive a catastrophe. Even after he moved to Bath as missioner, in 1817, Baines was involved in the school, and it was precisely the same educational theories that he wished from 1830 to introduce to Prior Park. So in 1831, Prior Towers wrote to parents asking for their particular attendance at the annual order of examinations 'in order to form their own unbiased judgment of the progress made by the students during the last year . . . of peculiar and extraordinary difficulties for the establishment'. Later in the same letter, Towers expressed his hope that:

Parents, taking into consideration the obstacles which have been surmounted, will not only find reason to be satisfied with the attainments of the last year, but will also from them receive a pledge of success.

It is difficult in the years between the departure of Baines and the developments of Prior Cooper to gain a clear sense of how the school was able to maintain its academic standards. Certainly the principle of breadth of studies did endure, and other features of school life like the annual examination probably did continue, although there are gaps in the records that survive. During Prior Cockshoot's terms of office, we sense a growing confidence in the education being offered, with perhaps more emphasis on the classics than had been the case earlier. The most decisive change in the second half of the century came with the adoption of the public examination system favoured by the public schools, a decision made by Prior Anselm Burge from which the school has never looked back.

Away from their desks

Schooling at Ampleforth was something that parents and boys alike were encouraged to take seriously. The holiday was only a month long, so the boys spent the overwhelming majority of the year at Ampleforth. In a note to parents of 1820, the school authorities stated that:

> It is wished that parents would avoid as much as possible taking their children home, and on this account there will be no additional charge to those who leave them at college during the vacation: at other times no student can be allowed to leave his studies and parents are requested not to ask it.

In the early decades of the school, it seems that the liturgical life of the Community formed the backbone of the non-academic activities for the boys. Feast days were marked by additional play time, and when this was cancelled the boys felt aggrieved. Religious activities remained important throughout the century, and the school rules are especially specific with regard to the saying of the Angelus. During study time, this was to be led by the master in charge, but during recreation it was led by the senior boy present. Boys who were outside, whether on the Bounds or elsewhere, were expected to recite it in private. Other religious activities included processions, May devotions which were started in 1844 and an annual retreat. The first of these appears to have been in 1850, and was lead by a Fr Rinolfi. A series of handwritten notes survives, detailing the times and places of silence during this period.

The Ball Place, final position, c.1880. Giles Gilbert Scott said of it, 'Of all your buildings I like it best.'

Attendance at Mass was, of course, integral to the life of the school. Boys were expected to serve at Mass and could receive a punishment if they were late. At the Sunday Mass, Catholics from the locality also attended, at least before the establishment of the local parishes. Indeed, before 1830 it was the custom that the village children received their religious instruction at the altar rails immediately before Mass.

The schoolboys did not spend all of the rest of the time at their desks. The first play was produced at Ampleforth on the night of 21 February 1814, a performance of *Julius Caesar* followed by a Molière farce. The same pattern was repeated in 1827, with a performance of *Henry IV part 1* and of Molière's *Les Fourberies de Scapin*. In that year, the programme included the note, 'The students hope their juvenile endeavours may meet with indulgence'. The earliest plays formed part of the annual festivities that preceded the season of

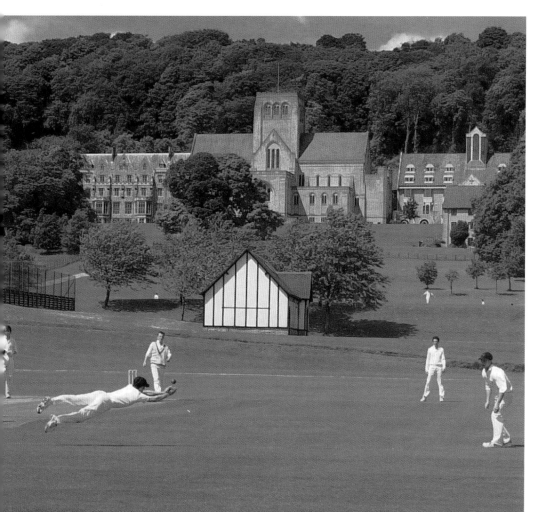

Cricket today, the 1914 Pavilion on the left.

Br Benet McEntee.

'The match was won for the loss of one wicket', W. Lambert, right, 282, O. M. Williams 119, both not out. First XI victorious over Gilling, 1902.

Lent. It was in 1827 that they moved to the Exhibition, and thereafter they flourished. In 1848 there were six different plays, with some actors appearing in four of them.

The first evidence of music for performance is also in the 1827 programme. It refers simply to a band, which by 1853 had become the Students' String Band, able enough to put on a performance of pieces by Haydn. However, the musical scene seems to have been dominated by the production of operas, which from the mid-century were directed by Herr von Tugginer of Leipzig. Some of these were original compositions, and Fr Cuthbert Almond speaks of a production of the operetta *New Boy* in 1863 'whose songs remained long in the memory', for reasons unstated.

The earliest outdoor games were not organised sports, although there is evidence of a ball place existing from very early on. This sort of game may be a survival of a French tradition, and similar structures to the Ball Place are found at Downside, St Edmund's Ware, Stoneyhurst and Ushaw. The first evidence of cricket dates from 1864, and the scorebooks from this period survive. The first pavilion was constructed about 1875, and the first swimming pool in 1880. This was in fact a reservoir, built on the top of Aumit hill, and a dedicated pool was constructed ten years later, near the site of the current top tennis courts. It was an unsatisfactory piece of work, collapsing almost immediately, perhaps due to the tendency of the land there to slip gently towards the valley floor, so a third pool was built around 1895, to the east of the pavilion. By this time, there is also plenty of evidence of football being played, with teams made up of boys and monks formed to compete with local villages. Compulsory sport was introduced by Prior Burge. Association football was introduced and played by the whole school; cricket, under professional training, was brought to a higher level; athletic sports became an annual institution; and swimming competitions began.

Outings to places of local interest were part of school life from very early on. There were trips to Newburgh and Byland, and we hear of a special outing in 1845 when the school was taken to see the Queen during her visit to Castle Howard. It was noted that 'to walk upwards of 20 miles to greet Her Majesty was no mean proof of Catholic loyalty', although all the boys saw was her carriage driving through the park. Unfortunately, the zeal of those responsible for the outing led to an error – the boys cheered the first royal carriage they saw which turned out to contain only a duchess. The second carriage, which passed by without a cheer, in fact contained the Queen.

An alternative location for those seeking a break from studies was the infirmary, which for much of the century was presided over by the legendary lay brother, Br Benet McEntee. A handwritten description of life in the infirmary describes how one boy, while lying on the sofa in order to allow his medication to take effect, watched the comings and goings of boys and monks. At seven in the morning, he says that ten or twelve boys were waiting for attention, beginning with one who had a sore thumb from a thorn. Br Benet's response to this ailment was straightforward:

He put his hand into his pocket, pulled out his lance and gave his thumb a cut. The boy then began to shout out: 'Bennett, Bennett, you are hurting me!' then Bennett began to squeeze it, and made the boy shout harder, and harder, 'I shan't come to you again with a sore thumb'. So Bennett turned him out.

30

Other boys came with more serious complaints, though few were lucky enough to gain the prize cure, an ample supply of toffee. Bennett sent some straight to bed, but only those who did not want to go there. We hear of a boy with a painful ear who was told to stay in bed, but did not get any toffee to enjoy there. Frequent complaints about the taste and quality of the medication prescribed are reported, although, as the anonymous author of the piece makes clear, 'you must admit of a few exaggerations'.

Rugby First XV, 1922, 12 out of the 16 here have colours. Captain T. M. Wright.

These anecdotes of the infirmary are found in a school magazine entitled *Hours of Leisure*. The tradition of school literary endeavour started in 1814, and after 1846 many different titles appeared, of which the most enduring were the *Collegian* and *The Student*. This latter in particular was a remarkably ambitious publication, treating of English and foreign literature, philosophy and contemporary issues such as evolution, heredity and positivism. There are complex criticisms of the writings of Burke and Lord Macaulay, all written by boys. This habit of writing continued after the *Student* ended its life in 1854; it was replaced by the *New Collegian*, the *Pantathlon*, the *Ruby* and many others. While we cannot be certain how much of their content was at the boys' own initiative and how much was under the guidance of their teachers, they bear witness to a remarkably thoughtful culture.

Most of these magazines disappeared in the mid 1880s. In their place appeared the *Diary*, a printed work devoted largely to recording the activities of the school term by term. It contains a wealth of detail about life in the school at the end of the century, with records of Exhibition performances, prize lists and a daily account of the comings and goings of the school and the monks and old boys. We read of the inauguration, on 15 November 1892, of a new institution, the 'smoking concert', for friends of Ampleforth and Old Boys in Liverpool. The idea had come from Fr Athanasius Fishwick, the honorary secretary of the Ampleforth Society, and, as he was in Liverpool at that time, Prior Burge presided over the evening. A week later, to mark the Feast of St Cecilia, a special holiday was arranged at Ampleforth. The next day another celebration marked the Prefect's feast, when all the boys went out for walks and then gathered for dinner and a magic-lantern show. An attempt was made at a bonfire, but, it being November at Ampleforth, everything was far too wet.

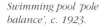

Swimming pool 'pole balance', c. 1923.

The successive volumes of the Diary also contain the accounts of sports fixtures which have since become a feature of the *Ampleforth Journal*. On 29 November 1893, the football team travelled by train to Pocklington for an important fixture, a return match demanded by Pocklington after Ampleforth had trounced them six–nil. This return game was a draw at 2–2, though perhaps the Ampleforth team was handicapped by the fact that they had left the bag containing their football boots on the train. Pocklington gladly supplied them with replacements, 'but several failed to get boots to fit them comfortably, and as a consequence were lame'.

The *Diary* shows awareness of a world beyond the valley as well. Each edition contains a summary of 'Benedictine News', including notes on the Ampleforth parishes and other monastic foundations in Ecuador and Brazil. Amazingly, the frontispiece of the Diary for Christmas 1893 is a portrait of the Abbot Primate of the Benedictines, Hildebrand de Hemptinne, whose visitation to the Congregation a few years later was to be the immediate precursor to the elevation of the monasteries to the status of abbeys.

5

The Monastery and its Parishes *up to 1900*

The huge achievement of Priors Cockshoot and Cooper bore fruit in the last 40 years of the 19th century, a period of steady and confident expansion both at Ampleforth and on the missions. In 1850 the Community numbered 48 monks, and 50 years later this number had almost doubled. At the same time, the missionary work undertaken by the monks grew rapidly as the Catholic Church in England attempted to keep pace with the staggering growth of industrial cities and their poor Catholic populations. These years also witnessed a slow gathering of pressure on the Congregation, still structured in 1850 as it had been in 1650 according to the needs of a missionary work on enemy territory. The last years of the century saw this pressure boiling over into change, culminating in 1900 with the election of Abbots of the three new Abbeys.

The high point of the missions

The last decades of the 18th century had witnessed a slow but real change in the popular perception of Roman Catholicism in England. It was still regarded as suspect, and strongly associated with Roman expansionism, but it was no longer seen as a threat to the stability of the realm. Most of the laws discriminating against Catholics were not repealed until 1829, but they ceased to function many years before, and during the crisis over emancipation they were more symbols than real tools of judicial persecution. In response to this, there was a gradual growth of confidence among the Roman Catholic body at large, and Catholic churches started to appear in settings which would have been unthinkable 50 years before.

This process of transformation is clearly visible in the story of the foundation and growth of the Easingwold mission. In 1794, the Laurentian Fr Jerome Coupe moved his home from a recusant household to Crayke and established a place of worship at nearby Oulston. In 1827, Fr Cyprian Tyrer, another monk of St Laurence's, received permission to move this mission to Easingwold, where he built first a small house and then a church. This church was designed by Charles Hansom, one of the two brothers who later were architects for the new church at Ampleforth.

Above and below: *St John's, Easingwold.*

The early-19th-century missions in the north west were almost without exception touched by the influence of Fr Anselm Brewer, a larger-than-life figure of huge kindness but also of huge temper – somebody it was hard to miss on any occasion. In a letter to Prior Burgess, Fr Benedict Glover described how:

Anselm is here at present. He appears *in splendoribus* which has occasioned some remarks even in my hearing. I wish he had not been quite so splendid and . . . so fond of the splendid.

For all this, Brewer was undoubtedly a missioner of remarkable ability. After three years as an assistant at Edmund Street in Liverpool, he was appointed to the rapidly growing parish of Brownedge, which at that time is thought to have had one of the largest Catholic con-

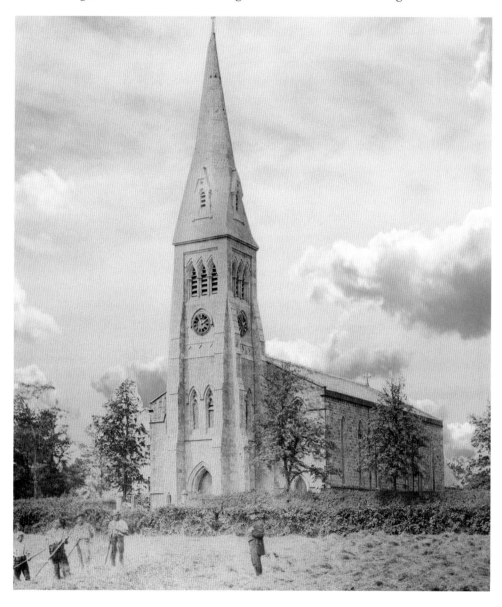

St Mary's, Brownedge (Bamber Bridge) before enlargement, c.1863.

gregations in the country. By 1827, he had already constructed a new church there, deliberately adopting the traditional form of an English parish church equipped with a tower. It was a bold statement of the confidence of Catholicism in the area. He was remembered at Brownedge as a fine preacher, effective in what he had to say, and uncomplicated in thought, since theological learning did not weigh him down too much.

He soon found opportunities for the establishment and development of missions beyond the boundaries of Brownedge itself. In the first place, he persuaded his superiors to establish a new mission at the village of Clayton Green, becoming Provincial of the North in 1837 – he used this post to extraordinary effect in pursuit of his ideals for other Benedictine missions in the region. New churches and presbyteries were constructed at Warwick Bridge, Birtley, Maryport and, most magnificently of all, at Edge Hill in Liverpool.

There are two epitaphs for Anselm Brewer's missionary career. The first, and now the most clear, is expressed in the great church buildings which he left behind, most especially that at Brownedge. It is a monument to the belief in the future of the faith that Brewer and his contemporaries espoused. On the other hand, his methods in achieving his goals were far from regular, and many weary years of conflict and discord absorbed the energies of the Congregation as it attempted to deal with what Brewer had done.

The second half of the 19th century saw the peak of this missionary endeavour . By 1865, 17 parishes had been founded in Liverpool, of which four were Benedictine, and as many of 50,000 Catholics were going to Mass in the city on Sunday. An unnamed Liverpool missioner recorded the work of ten Benedictine priests over the three main parishes, St Mary's Highfield, St Augustine's and St Peter's Seel Street. His estimate was that 7,320 people had received Communion in these parishes at Easter, and that huge sums of money had been spent or was being spent on the building of churches, schools and presbyteries.

A similar process of response to industrial expansion brought the Benedictines to south Wales. The population explosion here began in the first years of the 19th century, and in 1820 it was recorded that 300 Catholics lived in the town of Abergavenny. The first Mass in the industrial town of Merthyr Tydfil was probably in 1824, and by 1843, there was a regular Mass for the 700 Irish Catholics living there. Conditions remained dreadful, and the town had no adequate church until 1894. Rather, Mass was celebrated: 'in a dark, low loft, without ceiling, beneath which is the foul, noisy public slaughterhouse of the town'. The first Benedictine involvement in Merthyr was in 1851, when Fr Placid Sinnott arrived to take over the work. He remained there for 14 years, during which time he built both a school and a hall in which Mass could be celebrated. The Benedictine presence resumed in 1878. Fr Stephen Wade built the priory house and then in 1894 opened Merthyr's first church, built by the same Joseph Hansom who had been architect for the church at Ampleforth.

No part of the English mission remained unaffected by the changes that overtook Victorian England. Similar stories can be told of monk missioners in Warrington, Workington and throughout Lancashire. Yet this success brought with it its own pressures, for not only the missions were experiencing a new sense of confidence and purpose. The monasteries too were changing, though more due to pressure from without than from within.

Reform Imposed

In the period after the resignation of Prior Cooper, Ampleforth experienced a curious mixture of expansion and instability. The school and the monastery continued to grow in

The church at Merthyr Tydfil, completed 1894.

Monks' choir stalls in Hansom Church, photographed before 1901.

35

number, with the novices and juniors undertaking their studies at the Congregational House of Formation at Belmont. Yet from 1863 to 1885, the General Chapter found it hard to elect a Prior of Ampleforth; in these 22 years, there were five successive superiors, only one of whom lasted longer than six years.

In 1885, unusually, the Community elected Anselm Burge, the last of the great figures of 19th century Ampleforth. It is to Burge that many of the most important changes in the history of the Community can be attributed, not only at Ampleforth but also on the missions and especially in the foundation of St Benet's Hall.

Anselm Burge had come to Ampleforth as a boy during the last years of Prior Cooper's tenure, and in many respects he followed on from where Cooper's developments had left off. His first concern was education, and it was significant that he had spent four years teaching away from Ampleforth at the school run by Mgr Lord Petre at Woburn Park near Weybridge. As First Prefect, he introduced to the school the Oxford local examination system, realising the need for the school to take its place in the wider world of education. As Prior, he continued to be closely involved in developing the school, encouraging further the adoption of public examinations as well as establishing compulsory games. In more ways than one, Burge's reforms of the school anticipate the changes that were to take place in the 20th century under Abbot Edmund Matthews and Fr Paul Nevill.

The link between them is more than coincidence. The latter two were able to take advantage of the opportunity to study at Oxford, as established by Anselm Burge. The opportunity to educate young monks at Oxford was one of the most powerful catalysts in the transformation of the school, and shaped the future of the Community as a whole, as will be seen in a future chapter.

Burge also perceived a need to redevelop the monastery itself, and he conceived the building of a new monastery on a grand scale. In 1890, he began the process of discussion within the Community, which led in the end to the appointment of an architect, an old boy called Bernard Smith. His original plan involved the rebuilding of the whole of Ampleforth,

Monastery cloister.

with a four-sided cloister for the monastery and, between this and the school, a new Gothic church with an immense spire more than twice the height of the current church tower. One can only marvel at the scale of the vision, and something of its spirit remains in the only part of his plan ever to be completed, the main monastery building. This was designed to accommodate some 40 monks, with space in the basement for lay brothers, although Ampleforth never had more than a very few of these.

This great vision was influenced by forces from outside the Community of St Laurence. At the end of the 19th century, the ideas of monastic reform initiated in France and exemplified at Solesmes started to have a noticeable effect on the thinking of some in the English Benedictine Congregation. Indeed, a concern for the reform of the English Congregation was evident in Rome from as early as 1854. Two issues lay at the heart of this: the structure of the English Congregation was

Monastery from below the Bounds.

looking distinctly out of date, and the relationship between the monasteries and the missions was seen as unsatisfactory.

The first moves towards reform began in 1881 with the Bull *Romanos Pontifices* on the relationship between bishops and clergy of religious orders in England and Wales. This sorted out some of the problems which had bedevilled the Church in England since the restoration of the hierarchy in 1851, but also inaugurated a general enquiry into the state of the English Congregation. In the summer of 1881, the Prior of Monte Cassino, Dom Boniface Krug, was sent by Rome as Apostolic Visitor to enquire into its true state, and Krug's eventual report was embodied in the Papal rescript *Cliftonien*, 1883. This called on the English Benedictines to revise their constitutions:

> to take account of the changed political and religious situation in England, and while retaining the missionary character of the Congregation should not lose the monastic spirit of St Benedict's Rule but rather maintain it in a more lively manner.

The Benedictine Medal of Monte Cassino, 1880, the 'norm'.

The response of the Congregation to this challenge was hesitant, so in 1889 a new Papal document *Religiosus Ordo* made clear what was wanted – urgent reform and renewal of the structure of the Congregation. Rome asked for the abolition of government by provincials, and for the placing of individual missions under particular monasteries. This represented a vast change, and a commission was set up to deal with the question of how to divide the missions. This involved difficult decisions about both personalities and property, and in the end Ampleforth took on 26 of the Congregational missions. Most were in Lancashire and

37

Liverpool, though others in Cumbria and south Wales, Yorkshire and even a single parish in Lincolnshire were placed under the Prior, who from 1891 was required to make his own visitations to these parishes and to appoint his own monks to serve in them. It was greatly to the credit of Anselm Burge that he managed this change with so little dissent from within his own community.

The change was nevertheless very great and so was the work involved in effecting it. In late 1897, the pressures of overwork and ill health forced Prior Burge to resign, and he left Ampleforth for the southern mission of Petersfield. After just a year he felt able to move to the hurly-burly of Liverpool, and for 30 years he took charge of the growing suburban parish of Grassendale. He was able to celebrate the golden jubilee of his ordination to the priesthood there in 1924, and died aged 83, still in Liverpool, in July 1929.

From Priory to Abbey

The pressure for reform of the English Congregation did not end with the transfer of the missions to the direct control of the monasteries. Some monks of the Congregation, especially at Downside, felt that the concentration of power in the General Chapter was too much of a brake on change, and others looked more towards the monasteries and to the celebration of the liturgy as the direction which their lives should take. Outside the English Congregation, other things were changing. In 1872, the Community of St Augustine's at Ramsgate, belonging to the Subiaco Congregation, celebrated the blessing of the first mitred Abbot in England since the Reformation (an Old Boy of Ampleforth), and elsewhere in the country other monasteries formed in the continental tradition were becoming established. In 1895, a further Roman visitation to the English Congregation took place under the Abbot Primate of the Benedictine Order, Hildebrand de Hemptinne. This led to the issuing of *Diu Quidem* in June 1899, under the authority of which new Constitutions were written. At the heart of this last Papal document was the requirement that the communities should elect their own Abbots.

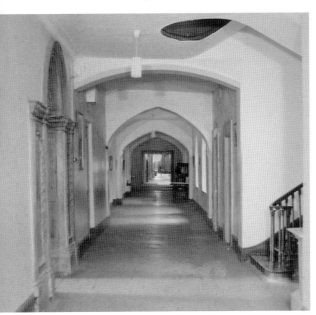

The Bell passage, looking from the Old House towards the Monastery. The Monitors' Room is on the left.

The reaction to all these changes was huge, divided and at times extreme. A great responsibility lay with the President of the Congregation, Anselm O'Neill. Strong voices were raised against change, whereas voices in favour of change were heard especially from within the resident communities. Overall, it seems that monks of Ampleforth were content to have the decision taken out of their hands by the intervention of the Holy See.

When Burge resigned in 1897, the Community elected a very different man to replace him, indeed one of his principal opponents. Fr Oswald Smith wanted an altogether slower process of change, although in a few short months he replaced every official whom Burge had appointed. In 1900, Prior Smith was blessed as the first Abbot of Ampleforth, an event celebrated by the *Ampleforth Journal* with an article by the now elderly Bishop Hedley, entitled simply 'On Abbots'.

Hedley had foreseen this change as early as 1886, no doubt reading the writing on the wall of Rome. For him, the election of English Abbots in the English Congregation was proof of the growth of the Benedictine Order throughout the world, and it was certainly a powerful sign that the first duty of the new Abbots was to go to Rome for the dedication of the church of Sant Anselmo, the international Benedictine House of Studies established in 1884. Oswald Smith's blessing as Abbot on 3 October 1900 was reported by the Tablet as the natural conclusion to the restoration of the hierarchy of bishops in 1851. The *Ampleforth Journal* declared that:

> No one living has ever seen, and perhaps no one living will ever have the happiness to witness again such a gathering of the brethren . . . brothers in one-hearted devotion to their gracious mother . . . who has, in the truest sense, renewed her youth, transformed from an old priory into a young abbey.

It marked the end of an era, but it was not the end of change. Although Anselm Burge was by 1900 already a successful parish priest in Liverpool, the transformation he effected at Ampleforth was to have an impact lasting many more years.

St Austins, Grassendale, Liverpool.

Bishop Cuthbert Hedley

When Bishop Cuthbert Hedley died in 1915, the *Journal* declared that his 'work and career will ever be to us at Ampleforth one of our most treasured possessions'.

He joined the Community in 1854, when the impact of the changes made by Priors Cockshoot and Cooper was beginning to be felt, and it was in a new climate of optimism that Hedley's monastic formation took place. He undertook his theological studies at Ampleforth, and in 1862, immediately after his ordination, he was sent to Belmont, the Congregational house of studies which had been established in 1859. For 11 years he taught there, not at all concerned to win a theological reputation, but 'determined to drive home the truth and to gain the souls of men'.

It was perhaps this quality that drew him to the attention of the hierarchy. In 1873, at the age of 36, he was appointed auxiliary Bishop of Newport, to assist the hugely influential Bishop Brown, also a Benedictine. This role did not occupy all of Hedley's time, and in these years he became well known as a retreat giver and as a preacher. In 1881 he succeeded Brown, and remained for 35 years as Bishop of Newport, until his death. The figures of his period in office reveal much about the staggering growth of Catholicism in the period. Over his 35 years, the number of Catholics in the diocese increased by 100 per cent and 53 new parish churches were built. In 1895, Rome acceded to Hedley's proposal to split the diocese in half, creating a new See of Menevia in the north.

Throughout his life, his devotion to Ampleforth remained profound. It had been Hedley who had composed an *Ode to Alma Mater*, that was sung at Exhibition for many years. In 1875, he was chosen as chaplain to the newly created Ampleforth Society, and it was Hedley who first suggested establishing a literary review, the beginning of the *Ampleforth Journal*.

Bishop Cuthbert Hedley.

6

Oxford

Of all the changes initiated by Anselm Burge during his time as Prior, none has had a more far-reaching effect upon the Community than the foundation of a house of studies in Oxford. Every generation of monks in the 20th century has been influenced by the experience of studying there, while the school depended for many decades upon the ready supply of Oxford-educated monks. This chapter tells the story of the involvement of Ampleforth in Oxford, and the foundation and growth of St Benet's Hall.

Returning to Oxford

Monastic communities have a long collective memory, and so when the first tentative steps were made towards establishing a house in Oxford, it was widely noted that this was not a beginning so much as a revival. The early history of the University was bound together with the needs of the great medieval monastic houses, who sought out Oxford first of all as a source of legal advice and secondly as a place of theological study. By the 15th century, five houses served the needs of monks in studies, both Benedictine and Cistercian, and there was a host of institutions for Friars and other religious. This structure of medieval theological learning was swept away at the Reformation, and until 1854 the Statutes of the University disallowed anyone from matriculating who would not subscribe to the Thirty-nine Articles of the Church of England. The change, when it came, was focused primarily on allowing members of the reformed churches, especially the Methodists, to attend the university. It was to be another 40 years before any Catholic institutions were to take root again in Oxford.

In fact, Catholics had good reason to be fearful of becoming involved in the universities. Their structure was Anglican, and those who knew something of 19th-century Oxford feared in addition that the prevailing atmosphere among the young was one of agnosticism rather than faith. A key figure in the process of change in attitude was Cuthbert Hedley, who at this time was Bishop of Newport. Hedley had once written that 'I would have given anything to be permitted to go to Oxford', and so when Rome consulted the bishops about the issue, he was in the forefront of those calling for change. He saw that there would be definite advantages in using Oxford, not especially for the training of priests but rather for the education of

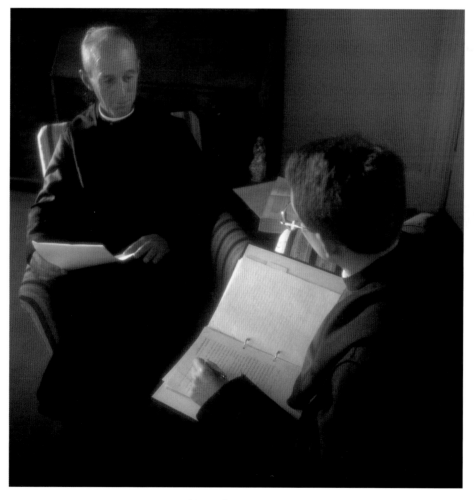

Tutorial at St Benet's.

41

the Catholic gentry which was important, 'because the Catholic status in the nation is dependent on them, and they are the source of our wealth and resources.'

Despite Hedley's enthusiasm, in which he was not alone, Rome decided in 1885 to refuse the request to change its position. It took another ten years before, in a decree of 1895, Leo XIII granted permission for students to attend the universities on the condition that a strong Catholic chaplaincy was established there, presumably to balance the prevailing Anglicanism of the university as a whole. This permission struck a chord with Anselm Burge, whose energy and vision found a natural expression in this new undertaking. It was in every respect a bright idea, as Burge later described in a letter of 1926:

> I think that I alone was responsible for the move. It was 'borne in upon me', and I held back for some time, as I found no one in my entourage to support me. In fact I think it was a special light from above which made me persevere. I was very ill at the time and very depressed and the opposition was very strong. How I held on to the idea I can never explain.

What was Burge trying to do? The Community of St Laurence has never had a tradition of academic activity, except in the circle around Augustine Baker in the 17th century and in the private interest of some individuals thereafter. The quieter corners of the English mission did enable certain people to find time for such work, such as Athanasius Allanson, but he is very much the exception among 19th-century missioners. Burge was not envisaging founding a community of scholars to pursue theology for its own sake. His focus was in fact very specific – a foundation in Oxford was justified because of its benefits to the school. He perceived that the future of Ampleforth College required monks with the proven ability and qualifications to teach. It is another sign of the remarkable perspicacity of Burge that he foresaw this need, and a witness to his strength of purpose that he achieved it.

There was certainly opposition to the scheme. Although it was clear to Burge that the future required this development, it looked, at least in the short term, like a threat. Some

Abbot Hunter-Blair, Fort Augustus, first Master.

St Benet's, 1959.

feared that Oxford would inevitably turn the minds of the young away from the urgent needs of pastoral work. Burge records that 'one good missioner at a public dinner prophesied that in ten years after Oxford the Community at Ampleforth would be a mere handful.'

There were all sorts of problems to face, even after the initial decision was taken. The first, and most pressing, was that the University's own laws required that any private hall should have a Master of Arts at its head, and the Ampleforth Community included no one with this degree. This required the Community to look elsewhere, and eventually a monk of Fort Augustus Abbey, Fr Oswald Hunter-Blair, was appointed. In 1899, he formally opened the new house of studies, named in the Oxford tradition as Hunter-Blair's Hall. In fact, groups of monks had been studying there since 1897, with Fr Edmund Matthews as their religious, if not academic, superior. With him in this first group were just three stu-

1947, Masters of St Benet's Hall, 1908–64: left to right, Fr Justin McCann, 1921–47, Fr Anselm Parker, 1908–20, Fr Gerard Sitwell, 1947–64.

dents: Br Elphege Hind, who spent just two years in Oxford before being recalled to teach in the school, and two postulants, William Byrne (later Fr Ambrose) and Stanislaus Parker (later Fr Anselm). This was as many as the Community could afford to send.

Fr Oswald Hunter-Blair was a remarkable figure, larger than life in every respect. A friend of Oscar Wilde while an undergraduate at Magdalen College, he is said to have acted as a stretcher-bearer in the army of the Pope during the siege of Rome in 1870, had abandoned strong Protestant traditions in his family to become a Catholic, and after joining the monastery of Fort Augustus had spent some years in Brazil assisting in the foundation of Benedictine communities there. He acted as Master of the Hall from 1899 until 1909, and was later Abbot of Fort Augustus. He continued to enjoy visiting Ampleforth throughout his life, and used to appear at the Exhibition wearing the special biretta granted to him by the Pope in recognition of his work in Latin America. The biretta was decorated with green, a mark of special honour, but it is recorded that no one at Ampleforth noticed.

The second difficulty facing the Oxford scheme was finding somewhere to live. For the first few years, the Community lodged at a house on the Woodstock Road, and then moved to a more central location on Beaumont Street. It was not until 1922 that the Community moved to its current home on St Giles.

Long before then, the first fruits of Burge's foundation began to appear. Edmund Matthews received his BA degree in 1901, remaining in Oxford to tutor other monks for two more years before being appointed Headmaster by Abbot Oswald Smith. The first Master of the Hall from within the Ampleforth Community was another of that first group of students, Fr Anselm Parker, although during his tenure the earlier custom of distinguishing between the Head of the Hall in the eyes of the university and a religious superior continued. In 1915, the question of giving the Hall a more permanent expression within the university was explored, and in 1918 both the Benedictine and Jesuit foundations were formally established as Permanent Private Halls. A University statute of that year granted this privilege 'on condition that provision has been made for the government of the Hall on a permanent footing, and that the Hall is not established for the purpose of profit.'

St Benet's Hall

The name of this new permanent part of the university was quickly chosen, St Benet's Hall. Its incorporation into Oxford was given physical expression when, in 1922, two houses on St Giles, formerly an Ursuline convent, were purchased. By this time, a new Master had also been appointed. In 1920, Fr Justin McCann had come to Oxford after just one year on the mission. He had been Prior of Ampleforth for three years before that, but was to remain at Oxford for a remarkable 27 years, the longest tenure of the post of Master to date. He supervised the purchase of St Giles, and he certainly left his mark on the way it was furnished and appointed. A man of very considerable personal austerity, the décor of the hall over this period was dominated by brown linoleum, and few of those who attended the hall in these years remember it as a place of comfort.

One reason for this may have been that the purchase of St Giles and the subsequent running costs of St Benet's were a considerable expense for Ampleforth. In 1928, Abbot Matthews admitted to Fr Justin that 'Oxford is a big expense on our revenues, and if it were not that the school is flourishing we could not meet it'. This was not to change until the 1960s. Throughout the period of McCann's mastership, St Benet's was a small community, comprised of monks and others religious training for the priesthood.

It fell to Fr Justin to look after St Benet's during the dark years of the Second World War. It seems that the burden proved heavy for him, such that Abbot Byrne wrote to him in 1943:

> You are doing an important, a necessary job, and doing it well. Far from being useless, you are filling a whole man's place in the scheme of things.

It is perhaps no surprise that, in 1947, a change of Master was made. Fr Justin, now honoured with the title of Abbot of Westminster, retired to the parish of St Mary's, Warrington, where he served as a curate and used his spare time to further his academic interests. The new Master was Fr Gerard Sitwell, who continued Abbot Justin's emphasis on scholarship, and quickly found Oxford a congenial milieu. He suited Oxford well, but it was nevertheless a surprising appointment. Fr Gerard had been responsible for the farm at Ampleforth for the previous seven years, and he had been noted for riding a horse on his journeys around the estate. Abbot Patrick, writing of Fr Gerard, says:

> He himself regarded the appointment with quizzical surprise. It took him from the tranquil concerns of the farm . . . to the comparative turbulence of academic endeavour.

In many respects, St Benet's did not change much over the 17 years that Fr Gerard was Master. Change did come, however, after 1964, when Fr James Forbes took over. It was during this time that St Benet's first started to admit large numbers of lay students, although the practice of admitting the occasional lay men dates back to 1948. Fr James was a character almost as large as the first Master of the Hall, and his lectures on porcelain within the university and the expansive generosity of his invitations are remembered in Oxford to this day. It has been written of him that

At the end of his time . . . there was no one in Oxford who was so widely known and so well loved. His was accepted everywhere.

Perhaps Fr James brought to St Benet's something of the same magic that also distinguished him as school guest master. It was part of his skill to make everyone feel welcome, and St Benet's gained a reputation for hospitality that it has never lost. The internal fabric of the hall was transformed at the same time, with the addition of a number of fine pieces of furniture that Fr James acquired, often gifts from the country houses of his friends. Fr James made it his business to represent one of Oxford's smallest permanent institutions at every level, discussing high issues in gatherings of heads of House, Dean and Senior Tutors, talking of money with Bursars and sharing essential practical wisdom in the meetings of Head Porters. Fr James was all of these – he also, as Abbot Justin and Fr Gerard had done before him, stoked the boiler.

St Benet's Hall.

Since then, St Benet's has continued to adapt to the rapidly changing world of higher education. Under Fr Philip Holdsworth, Fr Fabian Cowper and currently Fr Henry Wansbrough, the dual focus of the hall, upon monastic students and upon lay undergraduates reading for degrees, has been developed, and interaction between monks and the University has flourished at both the academic and social levels. Writing in 1997, at the celebration of the first centenary of the hall, Cardinal Basil Hume encapsulated the life of the Hall when he wrote:

Oxford has given much to our monks, and we are grateful for that. I like to think that our monastic presence in the university has made some contribution to it.

St Benet's Hall Today
Fr Henry Wansbrough

Oxford is a uniquely Christian city. The presence of so many ancient Christian foundations, visible at every turn in the centre of the city – and the virulently anti-automobile policy of the Oxford Transport Strategy makes walking or cycling the only practicable modes of locomotion – cannot but remind any visitor or local of its long Christian history. There is, I think, an unusually high proportion of church-going believers, each ancient College having its own functioning chapel, and a walk down St Giles' will convince that every branch of Christian or para-Christian ecclesial community has its conventicle in the city. Against this background, the monk in Oxford does feel himself to be the heir of a long and important tradition of monastic studies.

Over the last decades considerable changes have occurred in the Theology Faculty of the University. No longer a preserve of the Church of England, it now includes among its most respected members teachers of many different confessions. In the last few years a Catholic was appointed Professor of Ecclesiastical History (and a lay Canon of Christ Church). It includes also among its forty-odd senior members a Greek Orthodox Bishop, Baptists, Methodists, a Rabbi and over a dozen Catholics. The scientific and professional study of theology respects the confessional adherence of both teachers and students, so that it is possible for students of all faiths, and even of none, to engage without fear or embarrassment in research, study and dialogue. I have myself taught New Testament studies to two Jewish students. In this community of learning it is possible, and indeed enlightening and liberating, for Catholics to be taught by non-Catholics of many hues, and correspondingly for non-Catholics of many hues to be taught by Catholics. Certainly in biblical studies many tutorial sessions may pass without the ecclesiastical stance of either party coming to the fore – and equally without any danger of that Roman bugbear, 'indifferentism'. At the same time the study of theology is always a matter of personal involvement and development. There is a fair proportion among students of future ministers and of others who intend to devote themselves to some kind of church work, but also a large number of students who are simply fascinated and enriched by the study of theology and will make their way in finance, banking, management consultancy, the forces and the law.

In this theological endeavour the six Permanent Private Halls play an increasingly important part. This year the tiny St Benet's (45 students) is enrolling as many new theology students as any College in the university. It is a testimony to the vibrancy of Catholic life in this country that a surprisingly high number of theology students turn out to be Catholics, eager to examine and ground their faith in serious study.

The ever-increasing thirst at all levels of the Church for a serious study of the theological and historical basis of faith has also opened up pastoral opportunities for St Benet's. Fr Bernard and I have led study days and weekends at the Adult Education Colleges of both Oxford and Cambridge. St Benet's and its personnel are regarded as a resource in the diocese and beyond, providing day-courses for clergy and laity, readers, Eucharistic ministers, parish musicians and others. A particularly valuable annual feature is a week's scripture course for enclosed religious, monks and nuns – not only Catholics – who often have secular degrees and read the scriptures faithfully, but are precluded by their enclosed condition from any formal study. After the initial week of lectures (and general Oxford experience!) they return to their monasteries with a course-book and fax fortnightly essays for three months.

Another task in which St Benet's has contributed to the local and national Church is in providing chaplains to Catholic children in non-Catholic preparatory schools in Oxford, Summer Fields and the Dragon. St Benet's also provides a centre for monastic worship and prayer throughout the week, and – among the many menus available for the local Catholic – a sort of pseudo-parish on Sundays for a faithful, intelligent and challenging congregation of a few dozen.

However, St Benet's is not all theology. Two-thirds of the students are laymen. The work of developing mature and caring Christian laymen within a monastic framework, which is at the heart of the Ampleforth mission, continues at the level of tertiary education. By no means all the undergraduates are Amplefordian, in fact hardly more than one or two each year. Other Benedictine schools, the Oratory and Stonyhurst, contribute regular candidates, and this entry is broadened by a good admixture from maintained schools. When they leave, graduates have often remarked that they miss the feeling that the monks' celebration of the Prayer of the Church is sanctifying their day, whether they attend it or not. Academic standards are rigorous: over the past few years we have maintained a regular 15 per cent of First Class degrees, though the occasional Third cannot be denied.

In other ways, too, St Benet's can hold its head high in the wider sphere of the university. There is a regular smattering of Blues in various sports, and representation in the international debating teams of the Oxford Union. The Christ Church Beagles draw their Master from the ranks of St Benet's undergraduates with a surprising frequency, and St Benet's solitary VIII inches its way doggedly up the tables ('The monks have bumped, the monks have bumped, the monks have bumped', went up the cry on the bank at the end of one particularly hard-fought test). In a famed David-and-Goliath contest the St Benet's team successfully confronted the hordes of the Open University in 'University Challenge'.

Fr James Forbes, Master, 1964–79.

7

Creating the Modern College

The Rise of Ampleforth College
Peter Galliver

The association between Fr Paul Nevill and the rise of Ampleforth within the world of the English public school is well known. Fr Paul's work, however, was built upon foundations laid by Fr Anselm Burge and Fr Edmund Matthews. Fr Paul readily acknowledged the important role played by Fr Anselm Burge in the development of Ampleforth. In correspondence with the Cambridge don, H.O. Evennett, he wrote:

> The man who ought not to be left out of any account of Ampleforth's develop-ment is Prior Burge. He was the real instigator here of school reform and his ideas had their inspiration from Lord Petre and his experiment at Woburn Park. Moreover, he founded the Oxford House, St. Benet's Hall and it was he who sent Abbot Matthews there to start it.

Fr Anselm Burge, however, was not able to see his initiatives through. The move to transform the school into something which could meet the demand for a Catholic school organised along the lines of the leading English public schools, and working to their academic standards, was a matter of contention within the Community.

There was a conservatism with regard to the school, particularly on the part of many of the monks engaged in work on the parishes of the Ampleforth missions. The school which had produced them, and men like Bishop Hedley, whatever his subsequent enthusiasm for change, did not seem too bad a place, especially when the changes being proposed would have brought Ampleforth more into line with Protestant schools. The Catholic tradition in secondary education was one in which boys were organised by year groups rather than houses, where disciplinary powers were in the hands of masters rather than prefects, where the activities of students were fairly closely monitored and where the curriculum extended beyond the classics. This was a world away from the Anglican public schools with their organisation based on powerful headmasters, houses, professional laymasters, prefects with considerable disciplinary powers, fagging and a commitment to the cult of games and athleticism.

Coming into the 20th century, Ampleforth was a school very much in the distinctive Catholic tradition. There was no headmaster and no housemasters. The school was run by a Prefect of Studies and a Prefect of Discipline. Boys were taught by young monks. Normal practice was for a monk on being ordained to leave the school and to go out from the monastery on parish work. The school still played sports derived from its time in continental exile. There was no great desire in the Ampleforth Community as a whole to see things change too much.

In the Ampleforth context, moreover, there was the matter of balance between school and monastery. The monastery had always dominated the school; in many respects the school was part of the monastery. While the school had from early on included lay boys it was still the place that formed members of the Community. Before Fr Edmund Matthews built up the sixth form just before the Great War, most lay boys left at 15 or 16. Those who stayed on remained because they intended to pursue a monastic vocation. A school of two hundred plus, organised into houses, a

Ampleforth Abbey and College (1978 picture), compare with page 77.

Fr Paul Nevill, 1952.

school that would imitate the Anglican public schools and which, if it were to compete successfully in the gaining of entrance awards at Oxford and Cambridge, would probably need the introduction of well-qualified lay masters, would throw the balance of Ampleforth. There was an anxiety that an expanding English public school on the site at Ampleforth might come to distract the Community from its focus on the monastic life and tradition of service to the parishes; a fear that concerns about school affairs and housemasterships would assume too great an importance.

Fr Anselm Burge, therefore, was unable to do more than provide the opportunity for young monks such as Fr Edmund Matthews, Fr Paul Nevill and Fr Placid Dolan, to study at Oxford and to sow the seeds in the minds of the younger Ampleforth monks of what the school might become. The beginning of change at the school had to await the appointment of Fr Edmund Matthews as its first headmaster.

That Fr Edmund should have been made Headmaster by Abbot Oswald Smith and given the opportunity to lay the foundations on which Fr Paul Nevill was to build is something of a surprise. Fr Oswald had been elected as Prior when there was a reaction within the Community against the direction the school was taking under Prior Anselm Burge. According to Fr Paul Nevill, 'Fr Oswald had been one of the greatest opponents of his (Prior Burge's) regime', certainly in its early stages. But by 1903 the fortunes of Ampleforth College were at a low point. Fr Cuthbert Almond had been able to write a centenary history of Ampleforth which showed Ampleforth having reached a peak coming into the 20th century. While this may have been true for the monastic community, recently raised to abbey status, it was not true of the school. The successes achieved by the school since the mid-19th century recovery under Fr Wilfrid Cooper seemed in danger of being lost. In 1903, the numbers had dropped to 78 and no boy in the school passed a public examination. Abbot Oswald Smith may have been reluctant to see Ampleforth College turned into an English public school, and may have been opposed to its rapid and excessive expansion, but he could not allow the school to close. The continued prosperity of the school was important to the Community. In a world in which Downside was becoming more like a contemporary Anglican public school and similar changes were being effected at Stonyhurst and Beaumont, Ampleforth was in danger of completely falling out of favour with Catholic parents able to afford boarding school education for their sons. Keeping Ampleforth entirely as it had been before the days of Prior Burge was no longer an option. In these circumstances Abbot Oswald Smith had to call on Fr Edmund Matthews, who took charge of the school with the new title of Headmaster; a significant step towards Ampleforth's structures starting to correspond with those of the wider public-school world.

As Headmaster, a natural caution, and the continuing conservatism of the Abbot and much of the Community, placed limits on what Fr Edmund could do with the school. In his time as headmaster the arguments for turning Ampleforth into a Catholic school which incorporated the best elements of the English public-school tradition could be rehearsed but could not be fully acted upon. The opportunity for airing the case for change was provided by the fiftieth anniversary celebrations of the school building erected while Fr Wilfrid Cooper was Prior. The principal

Ampleforth Abbey and
College 1900, *a drawing by
J. S. Hansom.*

speaker at the celebrations was the Bishop of Newport, Bishop Hedley, an Amplefordian. In his address he endorsed the ideas which radicals such as Fr Paul had been
pushing within the school and community:

> For real education there must be that continuous skilful guiding and piloting,
> without pushing or forcing, which makes a boy turn his acquirements into
> mental growth, and discipline his own mind, heart and soul. To achieve such a
> result in a school, first, the boys must be left judiciously to themselves; secondly,
> the masters must forbear from taking too much notice of them; thirdly, the bril-
> liant boys must not be made too much of, and the average ones must never be
> neglected; and lastly, cramming and feverish work for examinations should be
> carefully kept down, for work of that kind runs off mind and character like a
> shower of rain from the roof.

The Bishop's address was published in the *Ampleforth Journal* of 1912. Alongside it
were two major articles by Fr Edmund and Fr Paul. Fr Edmund wrote on 'The Ideal
of Catholic Education', and Fr Paul on 'Liberty and Responsibility for Boys'.In his
article Fr Edmund reminded parents of the importance of a Catholic education:

> If, then, there is this Catholic atmosphere of religious truth and moral virtue,
> those parents take on themselves a grave responsibility who neglect to avail them-
> selves of it, and who put their children in a non-Catholic atmosphere in their
> school life. If ever there was any force in their plea of the importance of social
> caste, it has grown weaker as the Catholic schools have developed, and, more-
> over, there is no benefit that can outweigh the good of a Catholic environment.

He went on to acknowledge the growing demand for a public-school type of education to be made available in Catholic schools and to argue that this was being
achieved, without damage to Catholic educational traditions:

Abbot Edmund Matthews, 1924–39.

Some parents would urge that they are anxious to secure the 'public school' type of education for their boys, the manly independence and sense of responsibility that is associated with the name of Arnold of Rugby and the system that he has made popular.

In his paper Fr Paul went beyond Fr Edmund and made a plea and justification for the full-scale switch to the house system:

It is now generally realised that English Catholic boys cannot be brought up on a system that is really continental in origin and in spirit. Still more important is the fact that Catholics are no longer regarded as pariahs by their fellow countrymen, that they now find their way as a matter of course to the universities, into the army and the civil service, and are daily called upon to take up important positions and fill important posts . . . By liberty is meant that in the out of school hours there is no immediate supervision of boys by masters. No master watches over them in their playing hours, but they are left to themselves, bound by few and necessary rules, which ought to become less in number as they grow older, and the observance of which is made a matter of personal honour and trust among the boys themselves . . . The evils that supervision attempts to meet would be largely met by the adoption in our Catholic schools of the House System. The main difficulties of boarding schools come from the herding of boys, or the barrack system, and this is best remedied by the adoption of the House System, which gives all the advantages of a big school, and allows for the play of all those good influences which come from a small school. The best argument for the argument here advocated is the sense of mutual distrust and the consequent habit of evasion which the system of supervision breeds.'

The adoption of the house system and most of the other changes which were to see Ampleforth develop as a leading English public school had to wait until the election of Fr Edmund Matthews as Abbot and his appointment of Fr Paul as Headmaster in 1924. What Fr Edmund was able to achieve as Headmaster, however, was a significant shift in the school's academic standing, the beginnings of the monitorial system, and a demonstration that change could be for the better. He gave Fr Paul a solid foundation on which to build.

A valuable insight to Ampleforth during the first part of Fr Edmund Matthews' time as headmaster is provided by a memoir written by Brigadier Noel Chamberlain. As one of the boys who lived through the beginning of Ampleforth's transformation, and who became the College's first head monitor in 1912, Chamberlain remembered:

When I went to Ampleforth (in 1906), it was a small school of about 130 boys. This was not its only shortcoming. There were only three lay masters, including the part-time Arts Master, the Music Master and the Science Master. The remainder of the teaching was done by monks, few of whom had adequate qualifications. Another shortcoming was that the ages of the boys ranged from 10 to 18. In point of fact most boys left when they were 17 or even 16, so, when I went there in 1906, Ampleforth had no Sixth Form in the true sense . . . He [Fr Edmund] became Headmaster when Ampleforth was a small, badly taught and unknown school. By the time he died it had become a large, well-taught and well-known school. To him must be given the credit for this great achievement.

The success of Fr Edmund's regime can be seen in the recovery of school numbers. In 1919 the College had 200 pupils. The rise in the standard of scholarship was seen in the College beginning to compete successfully for awards at Oxford. Oxford-educated monastic teachers such as Fr Paul, a historian, and Fr Placid Dolan, a mathematician, were able to set an example for their fellow monk teachers to follow and to give directly to the boys of their expertise. Ampleforth had sent a few boys as commoners to Oxford once the prohibition on Catholics attending the ancient universities was lifted, but in 1912 scholarships began to be won. Vincent Narey won an open scholarship in history at Trinity in 1912. In 1913 he was joined at Oxford by Noel Chamberlain who had been awarded a history scholarship at University College, and Bernard Burge who had gained a scholarship at Merton.

Outside the academic curriculum, the major changes associated with Fr Edmund were a departure from having discipline exclusively in the hands of monk prefects by the introduction of monitors. For the first time at Ampleforth, boys were involved in the disciplining of other boys. The first Head Monitor, and Captain of rugby, Noel Chamberlain, remembered how this change had worked in practice:

Fr Paul Nevill, the painting, by Derek Clarke.

> There was no bullying at Ampleforth in my time. Until the monitorial system was belatedly introduced, discipline was maintained by three monk prefects, but of these only the first prefect really counted. There was corporal punishment. Usually it was not excessive but occasionally, in my opinion, it was . . . In my last year at Ampleforth the conventional British system of boy prefects or monitors was introduced. I was Ampleforth's first Head Monitor, and I did my best to do my job humanely and sensibly. No boy was beaten in my first term as Head Monitor. Discipline was not so good in my second term, so we had to make an example of the worst offender, rather a big boy who ignored the orders of a monitor given in the presence of some small boys. He took his punishment very well and showed no ill feeling towards us.

Fr Edmund's Ampleforth was a successful school, but, notwithstanding his emphasis on higher academic standards, some organisational change and admission to the Headmasters' Conference, it was still more recognisable as a Catholic college than a classic English public school. The school was full at around 200 boys, lacked the house system characteristic of the leading public schools and was still staffed almost exclusively by members of the monastic community.

Ampleforth, moreover, was still not widely recognised as a leading Catholic school. In some important quarters, however, there was recognition of what was being achieved under Fr Edmund. To the end of his life Fr Paul Nevill kept a letter which had been sent to him in 1916 in which the then Cardinal Archbishop of West-minster, Francis Bourne, was reported as saying to a visiting American bishop when asked to name the leading Catholic college in England, ' I think we must look to Ampleforth for the lead. They have quite the finest staff of any of our schools.'

Fr Paul
Fr Dominic Milroy

There are two well-known portraits of Paul Nevill. James Gunn's 'official' one, in the School Library, is accurate in every detail. That is what Fr Paul looked like, when in repose. But the most striking thing about his face, in real life, was that it was rarely in repose. His features, especially when he was speaking, were constantly and vividly mobile. The second portrait, the full-length one by Derek Clarke in the Main Hall, is not really a portrait at all. It is more of an 'impression' of Fr Paul as seen and remembered by countless boys. The impact of his tall and commanding presence is heightened by his being placed at a level several feet higher than that of the viewer. This captures, of course, the feeling of his most frequent encounter with the school en masse – morning prayers in the big passage; the hush that descended when Fr Paul appeared, like Moses coming down from the mountain, at the top of the steps; the collective shudder whenever he referred to some misdemeanour; the Edwardian turn of phrase which he imparted to his (infrequent) threats – 'If any boy were to be found guilty . . . He would most certainly be invited to continue his education elsewhere.'

Here again, however, there is something missing. This was not the real Fr Paul; it was simply the 'presence', sometimes terrifying, sometimes entertaining, always formidable, that he was able to turn on at will in public. He was in the same class as Winston Churchill (whom he hugely admired) when it came to public rhetoric. For the same reasons, he was, in private or semi-private, a marvellous raconteur, and, in the classroom, above all a vivid and enthralling 're-creator' of famous personages. His favourite was another great raconteur, Lord Palmerston.

The real Fr Paul, which was of course always coloured by this magnificence of presence and of diction, was the one that each boy knew in private. The school was never, for him, simply a crowd. His astonishing memory for names and faces extended, not only to each boy, but to their families as well. When he stopped a boy in the corridor, raised his eyebrows and enquired, with a huge smile, 'And how is your lady mother?', the boy knew that this was not just a way of being polite, but rather a real question about someone whom Fr Paul knew, and in whom he was gen-uinely interested. A prospective new boy, arriving with his mother to be shown round in the forties, and fearful of being interrogated by this immense man, was greeted instead by a broad smile, a funny story in broad Yorkshire and a birthday cake. Whether or not Fr Paul claimed (as he is so often reputed to have claimed on such occasions) that he made the cake himself, everything about his manner suggested that he had.

He had the remarkable ability to confer on each boy, on each guest, on each casual visitor, the gift of equality. This sense of hospitality was rooted in his carefully cultivated knowledge of who the other person was, and was deployed with invariable courtesy and humour. His style of conversation was deeply captivating. When he talked, his eyes lit up, his eyebrows moved expressively, and he had a very characteristic way of smacking his lips with delight whenever he said anything memorable or funny, which was usually every few seconds.

It goes without saying that, in the disciplinary context, it was no joke to be summoned by Fr Paul. However, he was not in the habit, in private interviews, of delivering spine-chilling harangues. He seemed to sense that the ordeal of waiting for the interview was punishment enough, and such interviews, whilst being on the bracing side, were usually conducted with genial eirenicism and were apt to be slated with illuminating comments about the meaning of life.

In all encounters, Fr Paul could be relied upon to be on the winning side. There were some rare exceptions. On the way into York one day, on the Reliance bus, Fr Paul found himself seated next to a boy. Assuming that the boy was on the way to the dentist, Fr Paul engaged him in cheerful conversation, in which the boy readily took part. On reaching York, they parted. Fr Paul went to his meeting, the boy to the station to catch the train to London. He was running away. This was not one of Fr Paul's favourite anecdotes. He would have been quite capable, however, of turning it into a parable of trust.

He was, by temperament and by conviction, an apostle of the centrality of trust. He believed profoundly that one should always trust boys, not because they were trustworthy but in order to make them so. This message was communicated by him in the grand manner and with a large measure of success. In return, he was perceived by the boys as a figure of heroic moral and physical proportions, and as an unforgettable model of sheer humanity on a big scale. Moreover, he never gave the impression of being a proud man. He was, palpably, a man of simple faith, devoted to his priesthood and his prayer, and a humble monk amongst his brethren. He carried authority effortlessly and lightly, exercised it generously, and penetrated it with an unquenchable sense of fun. He was born to be the creator and animator of a golden age.

*Fr Dominic Milroy,
Headmaster 1980–92,
by Marie-Claire Kerr.*

The birth of the school houses

As has already been seen, the idea of establishing school houses formed part of the far-reaching vision for reform laid down by Fr Paul in 1912. There is no evidence that this provoked an immediate debate in the Community, nor any evident hostility, for Fr Paul was made Sub-Prior in the same year, and in 1919 was stopped in the cloister by Abbot Oswald Smith, who, with characteristic distraction, mentioned in a casual way that he wanted him to be headmaster. Fr Edmund Matthews was at this point on holiday, but had been warned that he might be beginning a new life on the parishes from the autumn. Fr Paul considered this, but in a carefully worded letter to the Abbot stated that:

56

In the future development in a very conservative body of which we are members, Fr Edmund's advocacy and experience would be invaluable, and without which it is quite likely we may go back rather than forward.

In other words, Fr Paul perceived the need for Fr Edmund, widely respected and experienced, to continue the process of reform that he had started. This was indeed what happened – the Abbot was convinced and Fr Edmund remained headmaster until becoming Abbot in 1924.

In the intervening years, the awareness that a fundamental change in the shape of the life of the boys in the school began to grow. In 1920, Fr Edmund spoke eloquently in favour of some form of house structure at Ampleforth, and in the chapter of 1920 a proposal to build a house of 40 boys was passed unanimously. The architect Giles Gilbert Scott was invited to consider the options for siting such a building, and interestingly he first proposed a site

Bolton House, St Wilfrid's and St Edward's.

Facing page:
St Thomas's House.

57

known to later generations as Bolton House. Eventually, it was agreed to extend not to the east but to the west, although by 1922 other priorities for development had overtaken it. The building of the new church was clearly important, and Fr Bede Turner ensured that the installation throughout the campus of both electricity and central heating was given its proper place. Indeed, so important was this that the Exhibition of 1923 was cancelled because of the electrical work still in progress.

In 1924, as the new Church was taking shape, the issue of a new school house and development in general came back to the fore. Another discussion in chapter examined the concept of school houses as well as the ever present issue of finance, and the powerful arguments put forward by Fr Edmund carried the day.

Then Abbot Oswald Smith died, and Fr Edmund was elected to replace him. The wider implications of this are explored in a later chapter; for now all we need note is that this election, and the new Abbot's appointment of Fr Paul as headmaster, gave the necessary impetus to the development of houses that had been long waiting. By September 1926 the new house was ready, dedicated to St Cuthbert's and entrusted to Fr Sebastian Lambert, who was to remain there for 30 years. For the sake of convenience the remainder of the upper school were divided into three bodies under Fr Hugh de Normanville, Fr Stephen Marwood, and Fr Augustine Richardson.

These three houses, located within the main body of the school building, acquired a separate identity only gradually. Scott had managed to convince the Community that it would be possible to adapt both the Old House and the New College to meet the need, but in 1926 the necessary changes were in no way ready. The three houses shared the Study Block, with as much separation of dormitories as possible, but the sixth form all shared rooms wherever they were available.

Of the three, St Aidan's (until now) has moved least. St Bede's under Fr Hugh moved to the south end of the 'College' and the Lower Building where it remained until moving to Aumit Hill in January 1958. St Oswald's started life in the central area, and fully acquired its permanent home in the old house in 1933. There it was to remain until 1973, when it moved to Nevill House with St Dunstan's.

The early 1930s saw the establishment of three further houses as the school, under the leadership of Fr Paul, continued to grow. The first was St Wilfrid's, which began in the central area of the school, using as their common room the room familiar to later generations as the Memorial Library. It moved to the newly constructed Bolton House in 1933, in which year St Edward's was formed. This lived briefly at the east end of the Lower Building before joining St Wilfrid's in the new building. In 1935, the seventh school house came to being in the east wing of the old house. St Dunstan's, under Fr Oswald Vanheems, where it remained until the construction of Nevill House, with its sixth form occupying the top floor of the upper building.

After St Dunstan's, there were no new houses founded until after the war. St Thomas' under Fr Denis Waddilove started life where it has remained, acquiring a separate sixth form in Romanes House in 1949. This split site arrangement ended in 1981, when an extension was built to the original St Thomas', allowing the sixth form to return. In 1956, St Hugh's was started in a temporary building in the quadrangle under Fr Benedict Webb, and it moved to Aumit House along with St Bede's in the following year. This move enabled St John's to be born under Fr Benet Perceval in the newly vacated quadrangle building, but it soon moved into the old St Bede's in the lower building where, with variations, it has remained.

A reminiscence: Fr Stephen Marwood
Fr Adrian Convery

Fr Stephen Marwood at Goremire, c.1945.

By common consent Fr Stephen – or 'Steeny' as he was known to generations of Amplefordians – was exceptional. And yet it is not easy to put into words what it was that made him so special. He was respected – and even revered – by monks and boys alike. In 1952 Fr Paul Nevill, in *Ampleforth and its Origins*, wrote:

> Among the housemasters was a remarkable man, Fr Stephen Marwood. He had been, as a very young priest, the confessor of Abbot Smith, who saw in him a man and a monk after his own heart. Possessed of many gifts, he was above all a man of God. He proved himself the best teacher of boys that Ampleforth has had. He had the confidence of everyone with whom he came in touch, the Community, the boys – more especially his own house – and the servants. He was a power for good wherever he went, and any success the school has had must be largely attributed to him. Abbot Matthews set high store by his virtue and his views, and for a time he was not only housemaster, but both Sub-prior and master of juniors. It will be a long time before his like appears again.

Fr Stephen had been second prefect before becoming the first housemaster of St Oswald's in 1926. He died very suddenly in December 1949, aged only 59. In appearance he was short and stocky, with a very large square head, sparse, dark, straight hair, chiselled nose and features, small oval spectacles, and a massive jaw. He had a magnificent modulated speaking voice and could clearly have been a very fine operatic tenor – for he was a born actor. But if one single word could sum up his presence it would be the Latin *gravitas*. One never saw him hurry.

Paradoxically he was quite stern and a little remote and yet at the same time immensely understanding and human – one old boy writes, 'He combined sheer goodness with common sense and a great sense of humour'; Another says, 'Everyone thought him the best, and though he was distant, he was not'. Yet another says, 'In some ways one was always a bit frightened of him – even as Head of house one never got very close. Yet he was hugely admired and respected, and it was a feature of the house that it was so happy and friendly. Friendships frequently became lifelong, and it is striking how many remained practising Catholics'.

It is striking, too, that for all his many other gifts, Fr Stephen is still remembered above all else by so many old boys as a man of prayer and a man of God. And it is eloquent testimony to the power of his influence and witness that he was able to communicate this so vividly and without affectation to generations of very ordinary boys.

8

The Community and its Abbots

The election of Ampleforth's last ruling Prior in 1898 was a significant turning point in the history of the Community. For 12 years, the drive and energy of Prior Anselm Burge had brought radical changes in all areas of the life and work of the Community. His was a restless mind, always seeking the next project, whether the implementation of Roman decrees regarding the missions or the establishment of Ampleforth's own brick plant and the re-organisation of the water supply. By 1897, the Community had probably had enough. In 1898, a group of electors gathered at Malvern to meet with President Anselm O'Gorman, and the choice fell on Fr Oswald Smith. He had been Burge's most vociferous opponent, a man who could not have been more different in temperament. Elected Prior in 1898, Smith became the first Abbot of Ampleforth two years later, and was re-elected in 1908 and 1916. He remained in office at his death in 1924.

It is hard to tell the story of early-20th-century Ampleforth except through portraits of the men who shaped it. This was the age which exalted empire builders, and the monks who formed the modern Ampleforth were men of that sort. Through their lives, much more can be seen of the inner history and working of the Community than through bald facts of dates and buildings. This chapter will explore the history and dynamics of the Community through portraits of its first two Abbots, then the man who oversaw the expansion of the physical plant of Ampleforth, and then a monk whose life involved not only Ampleforth but its parishes. The parishes in this period will then be seen through the history of Warrington, where more monk missioners served than in any other town of the period.

Rightly, this chapter should of course include, Fr Paul Nevill, the father of the modern Ampleforth College. The extent and depth of his contribution has been treated in a separate chapter devoted to the transformation of the school in this period.

Portraits in a Landscape

In retrospect, the Ampleforth of the first half of the 20th century seems to have enjoyed a steady period of expansion. Certainly this is what the numbers suggest. In 1903, the Community numbered 96, by 1924 it had risen by ten and by 1939 to a total of 130. At the same time, the whole school (including Juniors) experienced an even more exponential growth, rising from 110 boys at the turn of the century to 250 in 1924 and to nearly 500 boys at the outbreak of the Second World War. This growth, especially that of the school, was by no means certain as the new century dawned. School numbers had been declining steadily during the last years of the 19th century, and it required radical steps to reverse this. Nevertheless, in this period we encounter a relentless optimism, the greatest legacy that Burge left to his Community when he departed for the Mission in 1897. He had somehow opened the doors of Ampleforth, moving beyond the safe but inevitably narrow world of an enclosed 19th century English Catholicism. The foundation of St Benet's Hall is an example of his willing-ness to take risks by exposing the Community and its works to a wider and a less securely Catholic world. Those who prophesied the decline of Ampleforth as a result of this policy had argu-ments on their side, but they were wrong. It was Burge's breadth of vision that allowed Ampleforth to recreate its school, and in a more imperceptible way to refashion the expectations and inner life of the Community.

This wider vision meant that events beyond the valley had their impact on the Community as never before. During the four years of the First World War, 64 old boys were killed in action, approximately equivalent to half the size of the school. Four monks served as chaplains in the forces, and some glimpses of the everyday heroism expected of people in that tumultuous conflict survive in their reminiscences. The prevailing sadness of that time touched the Community and all its parishes, from where so many young men left for Flanders.

Memorial Chapel screen, showing various soldiers from the Gospels.

On the brighter side, this new openness put Ampleforth into more contact with the wider affairs of the Church. Symbolic of this was the approach made to the Community in 1911 by the Bishop of Edmonton, Canada, who sought a school foundation for his diocese. The scheme was approved by the Community in its conventual chapter, so in October 1912 Fr Basil Clarkson and Fr Benedict McLaughlin set out for Calgary. The plan might indeed have worked, but for reorganisation of the diocese in Canada which led to the appointment of a new Bishop with new priorities. Despite the formidable negotiating skills of Fr Wilfrid Darby, who was sent to sort it out, the Bishop never gave a clear line on whether he wanted the foundation or not, so in February 1914 the monks returned.

Oswald Smith, Abbot 1900–24.

Two Abbots

It has often been noted that the Rule of St Benedict describes the Abbot using many different images. No two more contrasting models of this office could be found than in Ampleforth's first two Abbots, Oswald Smith (1900–24) and Edmund Matthews (1924–39).

When the Congregational electors chose Oswald Smith to replace Burge, they were making a conscious choice for someone very different. If Burge was a man of ideas, Smith was content to leave the daily business of governing a monastery and running a school to others, to concentrate on what he believed was more important, the practice of prayer and the preservation of unity within the Community. He had been clothed at the Congregational noviciate at Belmont in 1872, proceeded through solemn vows and ordination, and briefly taught in the school at Ampleforth. He did not shine in this environment, and seems especially to have had difficulty in dealing with the problems of discipline among the young. So he returned to Belmont in 1886 to teach philosophy. To this end, he spent seven months in Rome completing a doctorate, and he then taught for ten years at Belmont until becoming Prior at Ampleforth in 1898.

The new Prior made a lot of changes very quickly, and appointed Fr Edmund Matthews as Headmaster in 1903 and Prior in 1909 and Fr Bede Turner as Procurator in 1902, to whose work the post of Prior was added in 1919. In effect, as the Abbot he delegated the day to day running of Ampleforth to these two officials. He and those around him knew that details of administration were not his strength. In fact, his lack of grasp of day to day realities could be a source of immense frustration. He just did not see the task of Abbot in those terms, and, however weak his system might look from a managerial point of view, it must be noted that it worked.

We should not conclude from this that Abbot Smith was uninterested in what was going on around him. His tendency, however, was to place development second to the preservation of peace within the Community, and in this way he acted as a brake on the ambitious schemes put forward by the minds around him. Abbot Smith was remembered for his devotion to the liturgy that lies at the heart of monastic life. In 1922, Cardinal Bourne judged that Smith had done 'more than any other man of his day to give the celebration of the Divine Office its rightful place in the spiritual lives of secular priests'. He achieved this through his own example, his retreat-giving and above all through his published meditations, which communicate his essentially simple spirituality. After 26 years in office, Abbot Smith became an institution. Writing in the 1950s, Fr Paul Nevill said that, 'Abbot Oswald had become a habit of mind'.

He was hard to replace, and in some ways it was natural at his death to look for someone with different skills, with strengths in areas where he had been weak. The man chosen to replace him was indeed of a very different cast of mind. Edmund Matthews had been the first monk to receive a degree at the new Oxford house, and after two more years in Oxford he had been appointed the first Headmaster of the College in 1903. In this post, he had been one of Abbot Oswald's closest collaborators, and it is a sign of how much he was trusted that, in addition to his responsibilities for the school, he also held the post of Prior from 1909 to 1916.

The new Abbot's character was marked by a relentless self discipline – he is remembered for once expressing the question, 'What are laws made for, but to be observed?'. As Headmaster, he had established a strong school staff, relying for much support upon two monks whose loyalty and energy he admired, Fr Ambrose Byrne and Fr Sebastian Lambert. School numbers recovered such that, at his election as Abbot in 1924, the school was nearly 200 boys larger than it had been at his appointment as Headmaster. In 1907, an Oxford and Cambridge Board inspection had passed favourable comment on the school, and in 1911 Fr Edmund became the first monk of Ampleforth to be a member of the Headmasters' Conference.

His election as Abbot in 1924 brought no change in the steady growth that had been achieved under his predecessor. Significantly, the first religious ceremony over which he presided after his election as Abbot was the opening of the new choir, the first part of

Scott's plan for a new abbey church. Abbot Matthews immediately appointed Fr Paul Nevill to be Headmaster, but there was no fundamental change of direction from the policies that Matthews had been pursuing in the school. The establishment of the house system, was something that he had advocated as Headmaster, though he had always hoped that somebody else would have to face the practical difficulties of implementing it. Within the monastery, continuity rather than change was certainly the overriding approach. This was a period when individual monks held positions of responsibility for remarkably long periods of time: Fr Bede Turner was Procurator for 34 years and Prior for 16 years, and Fr Laurence Buggins was Novice Master for nine years (1926–35) before serving as Prior from 1935 to 1951. For more than 35 years, moral theology was taught to the younger monks by Fr Dunstan Pozzi.

Theatre under construction, 1909.

This was also a period of large noviciates; the noviciate returned from Belmont to Ampleforth in 1919, and by 1939 the Community had grown in size to 130. It had also changed in its geographical composition. The 19th-century Community had been largely drawn from Lancashire, whereas during the middle decades of the 20th century, the increasing number of boys coming from the school gave the Community a less solidly northern identity. There were more monks from the south, and some had close connections with the upper echelons of the Catholic gentry and nobility. To this extent at least, the shape of the Community was being re-formed by the new kind of school that Abbot Matthews and Paul Nevill were creating.

The growing importance of the school in the life of the monks had another important effect on the shape of the Community. In the 19th century, the number of monks who spent their whole lives in the house of their profession was very small, and all those who joined had a clear notion that part, often the greatest part, of their adult lives would be spent working on the mission. In the early decades of the 20th century, the missions still exercised a huge impact on the life of the Community, but the number of monks who spent their whole lives at Ampleforth increased as the responsibilities involved in running the school grew. Some perceived this quite early in the century, when the direction in which Edmund Matthews, then Headmaster, was taking the school aroused the opposition of certain mission

Upper Library, c.1900.

fathers. They feared, in some senses quite rightly, that the growth of the school in the way envisaged would have an effect on the number of monks available to work on the mission. By the middle years of the century, that prophecy was slowly coming true, and the balance of life in the Community was shifting slowly towards a larger resident community.

Abbot Matthews died suddenly on Good Friday, 1939. He had been ill for some two years, though it was characteristic of him to have made little of this. The only obvious sign of the state of his health was his quite unprecedented decision to take a holiday, something he never otherwise did. On Maundy Thursday he had sung the High Mass, and that evening he had spent time watching at the Altar of Repose. Early the following morning he died, and

Cartoons by Fr Sylvester Fryer; left to right: Frs Gregory Swann and John Maddox, Dunstan Pozzi, Raphael Williams and Abbot Smith.

it fell to Monsignor Ronald Knox to deliver the panegyric at his funeral. He identified his greatness as lying in the grace of being a father, concluding that:

> He was a great Abbot because he was a good monk . . . You saw, in that play of light and shadow, that this was a man whose thoughts were never far away from God. We shall not see it again; he has passed beyond our world of light and shadow; may the face of Jesus Christ show gay and gentle to him. You must turn, with heavy hearts, to elect another in his place. Reverend fathers, God send you a Father like him.

Abbot Bede Turner.

In their different ways, Ampleforth's first two Abbots relied upon members of the Community whose gifts were very different from their own. One man in particular played an enormous part in the growth of Ampleforth over this period. Fr Bede Turner, Procurator from 1902 to 1936, and Prior from 1919 to 1935, was a man upon whom rested the responsibility for the physical development of Ampleforth, and it was a task he fulfiled unstintingly. In his personal life, Turner was a man firmly attached to routine, such that Paul Nevill noted that 'his presence in one place or another was clear sign of what time of day it was'. He was a careful worker, a man in whose hands Abbot Smith placed both the details of day-to-day administration and the burden of executing a series of building projects. From his office by the archway, he planned first the building of a new infirmary, completed in 1909 and later transformed into the Procurator's office. In 1927, he constructed the present school infirmary, and supervised the building of the theatre, the larger cricket pavilion and the junior house. After the First World War, when the field to the east of the new college had been purchased, he supervised the building of the three new sides of the quadrangle, then Bolton House and the Upper Building. To the west of the monastery, he built St Cuthbert's and the south wing of the monastery containing a new library, Abbot's quarters and infirmary, which to this day is known as the New Wing.

In 1935 a serious illness forced him to retire, but he used his new-found leisure to great effect. He had always been interested in historical and theological studies, and he spent time in exploring the writing of St Bede, the geography of the neighbourhood and the records of the Lancashire Catholic families from which he himself had come. To the end of his life, he was responsible for instructing the novices in learning the details of the choir rubrics and ceremonial, for nothing escaped his notice even in church. On the day of his death, 24

November 1947, he had walked to the village and back, showing the same strength of character and determination of purpose that had marked all his immense achievements.

Perhaps equally influential, though in a very different way, was Fr Anselm Wilson. To the young Edmund Matthews, growing up in Burge's Ampleforth, Anselm 'Trainer' Wilson was a model monk, and as sub-Prior and Professor of Theology he had ample opportunity to put forward his vision of how the religious life should be lived. He was a man of unusual talents, retaining a lifelong interest in theology but also showing himself no mean poet. He regularly wrote an original prologue or epilogue for the annual Exhibition, and his poems were published in the *Ampleforth Journal* at regular intervals. When the rumour of his appointment to the missions spread, there was genuine consternation among the resident Community and especially among the young. But in 1893 he followed the path trod by so many monks in earlier generations, travelling from Ampleforth to Liverpool, where he served for 22 years at St Peter's, Seel Street. This was Ampleforth's poorest parish, serving communities of dockers in the city's teeming port, and in this work he exemplified the qualities of humanity and care for others which he had shown earlier in his life.

In 1917 it was felt that Fr Wilson needed a change from the arduous work at Seel Street. He was sent to Dowlais in south Wales, where his work among the mining community was

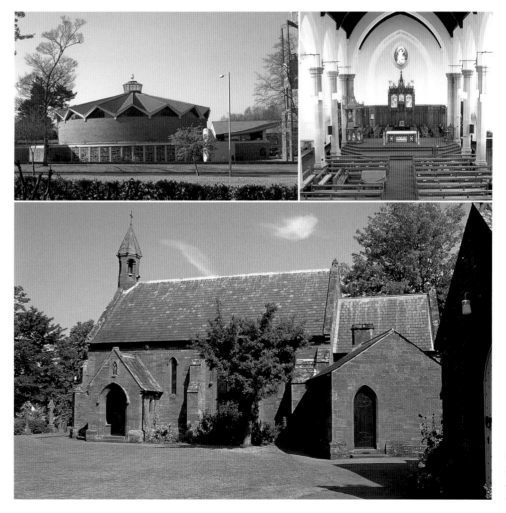

Clockwise from top left:
*Parish churches of Leyland,
Lostock Hall and Warwick
Bridge.*

challenging but less demanding. Nevertheless, in his nine years there, he rebuilt the nave of the church and erected a new school. Finally, he retired to Leyland in 1926, where the comparative peace of his life enabled him to resume his literary activities and complete the life of Bishop Hedley that had remained unfinished at the death of Fr Cuthbert Almond.

Anselm Wilson illustrates many of the currents that lie underneath the visible growth of Ampleforth in the first part of the 20th century. In his writing of the life of Bishop Hedley, he put forward a view which both subject and author shared, namely the integral connection between a life of prayer and the apostolic labour of school and parish. Anselm Wilson saw no distinction between these two, and he communicated to the young of the community an equal duty of prayer and work. His understanding of the monastic life allowed room for personal endeavour and even success among the young or among parishioners, but such success was balanced by an emphasis on personal frugality and asceticism and a devotion to private prayer which Wilson seems to have derived ultimately from the writing of Augustine Baker.

Fr Laurence Shepherd.

'The Athens of the North'

It would be easy to write the history of the Community in the first half of the 20th century as one of steady expansion in both monastery and school at Ampleforth. Yet this is to tell less than half the story, for throughout this period the missionary work of the Community on parishes continued to absorb a majority of the Community, as it always had done. The process by which the balance shifted slowly towards a larger resident community was slow, and Ampleforth went through none of the heart-searching that led Downside to abandon many of its parish commitments during this period. Although great change had taken place in the missions as a result of the papal reforms of the end of the 19th century, the missionary instinct endured.

It is possible to do more than glimpse the nature of this work, which required from the Community both regularity and profound personal commitment. This can be seen by examining the town in which was concentrated the largest number of missioners in this period. That town was Warrington, which at its peak could boast a dozen monks from Ampleforth, serving the four parishes that had been established by the mid-20th century. In the 18th century Warrington had been called 'the Athens of the North' because of its remarkable school, the printing press established there, and the foundation of the Warrington library, the forerunner of the modern public library. By the 19th century Warrington had become an industrial centre, creating in its wake new pastoral needs for the Catholic presence in the town.

Br Andrew Slater – lay brother who supervised the tiling and plumbing in the building of the Monastery.

The Benedictine mission to Warrington had long roots. The first priest to celebrate Mass regularly there was Fr Benedict Shuttleworth, a monk of Lamspringe, who came into the town from Woolston Hall, the ancestral home of the Standish family. They had retained Benedictine chaplains from as early as 1677, and from the mid-18th century these chaplains had taken on the care of the people in the growing nearby town.

Like any 18th century mission, there was always something impermanent about the Benedictine presence in Warrington in this period. Mass was celebrated in a series of public houses, and elaborate precautions were taken against detection by both priest and congregation. When Mass was celebrated at the Feathers Hotel in Bridge Street, each worshipper was required to carry a jug on his way to Mass, as if going to collect beer from the inn. The upper chamber where Mass was celebrated had a trap door in the centre, so that in the event of detection all present could jump through this on to a pile of sacks beneath. The hope was that, when the authorities arrived, the group would be mistaken for a party of sack menders.

The first priest to be formally assigned to Warrington was Fr Anselm Bradshaw, sent from Lamspringe in 1776. He established the first chapel, where in 1823, Fr Alban Molyneux built St Alban's church. At the opening of this powerful sign of Catholic presence in the town, the sermon was preached by Bishop Baines, who reminded those present of the Catholic past of the town, extending back to the Middle Ages. Just a few years later, indeed, Molyneux discovered a series of pre-Reformation vestments, which became one of the proudest possessions of the parish.

Abbot Austin Bury, builder of St Mary's Church on Buttermarket Street, Warrington.

As Warrington expanded in the 19th century, so the need for more parish churches became acute. In 1877 Abbot Austin Bury built St Mary's Church on Buttermarket Street, a massive Gothic church designed by the younger Pugin. In 1893, St Alban's was extended and adapted also by Pugin, by which time a new temporary mass centre had been established in St Benedict's school on Orford Lane. In 1902, St Benedict's gained its first parish priest, and two years later a temporary church was built to accommodate the growing parish. Finally, in 1927, a fourth Benedictine church was established at Padgate, dedicated to St Oswald and built at a cost of £3,500. Its founder was Fr Oswald Swarbreck, a much-respected missioner whose sudden death, just a few months after the church was opened, led to mourning throughout the town.

With large churches to serve, successive Abbots of Ampleforth appointed large numbers of monks to work in Warrington. The Community's link with the town become one of love as much as of service, as was recalled in 1927 when Abbot Matthews preached at the Golden Jubilee celebrations for St Mary's. Alongside him on the sanctuary was Fr Basil Feeny, who had as a young priest been present at the opening of that same church. The third (a fourth was added later) Ampleforth church in Warrington was opened in 1929, and the sermon preached by Fr Herbert Vaughan inevitably concentrated upon the Benedictine presence in the town:

> For over 200 years these zealous and apostolic men have laboured in the vineyard – laboured at the great work of reparation and restoration. Already they have erected two churches in the town, and today we are met together to celebrate the opening of a third – a church dedicated to St Benedict under whose auspices the faith was replanted in these parts.

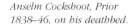

Anselm Cockshoot, Prior 1838–46, on his deathbed.

It is not easy to move beyond this to see in detail the work of individual missioners. Warrington was for many monks a first experience of parish work, in which they were educated by some of the great men of the mission. All the churches, schools and presbyteries required steady renovation and upkeep, and beyond this lay the essential but often invisible work of the parish priest, visiting and ministering to his community. We cannot now gauge the effect of this, except in the writings of the monks themselves, whose affection for the people of Warrington, and whose strong belief in the efficacy of their work, is a striking testament to the same sense of commitment that underlay the expansion of monastery and school at Ampleforth.

9

The Prep Schools

Ann Fairfax, who built Ampleforth Lodge for her chaplain, Fr Anselm Bolton. Painting by P. Mercier.

For many of the boys who came to Ampleforth from the second decade of the 20th century, and so for many of the Community drawn from them, the experience of Ampleforth did not begin at 13. An increasing proportion of the school started much younger, and could spend up to ten years being educated at Ampleforth. This chapter explores the development of prep-school education in the valley, and the distinct phases that culminated in the development of Gilling Castle as the prep school and the Junior House for boys from 11. It also tries to go behind the story, and to hear the voices of some of the boys who experienced prep-school education at Ampleforth in its early years.

The decision to go preparatory

The idea that Ampleforth should develop its own preparatory school has a long history. As far back as 1872, Prior Bede Prest had conceived of a scheme for founding a preparatory school somewhere in the valley, and during the time of Prior Burge, special attention was paid to developing the education of the youngest boys at the school. It was not however until 1908 that a distinct preparatory section of Ampleforth College was started, under the charge of Fr Aelred Dawson, the first monk given the title Housemaster. It had indeed always been the intention of Fr Edmund Matthews to develop in this direction, since he and those around him recognised a clear need. This was described some years later by Fr Paul Nevill:

> The existing Catholic preparatory schools in the south tended to dissuade parents from sending their sons to the savage north. On the other hand, many parents in the north were demanding a preparatory school for their boys.

The problem then was not whether a need existed, but how best Ampleforth should respond to it. The creation of a small preparatory department within the college, known as the Lower School, was one solution, but between 1908 and 1914 a variety of other options were given careful consideration. Principal among these was the possibility of establishing a prep school away from Ampleforth itself, which would act as a feeder school but would be located nearer

the intended market. In 1910, two properties in north Oxford and in Great Malvern were proposed to this end, and indeed the Abbot's Council accepted the principle, later in that year,
that either would be suitable should the permission of the Bishop be forthcoming. In the
Community Chapter that summer, the general idea of preparatory education was explored,
and investigations into possible options continued. Finally, at the Chapter of 1913 it was
agreed to establish a preparatory school somewhere at Ampleforth.

Once taken, there was several problems with this decision. The first was the location of
the new building: although space was available to the west of the monastery, there were
considerable arguments about the suitability of the site, such that the Abbot's Council held
a meeting in the proposed field to examine the preliminary holes that had been dug. Secondly, such a new building would be expensive, and there were not sufficient reserves at the
disposal of the Community to fund such a project without a substantial benefaction. In the
end, a bequest left by an old boy called William Taylor made it possible to begin operations,
although not before water and frost had so damaged some stone given for the building that
it could not be used. Work finally started in 1914, and continued under the shadow of war.
There were inevitable difficulties in working under these conditions, but the tenacity of
Bede Turner saw the project through to completion, and in 1916 the preparatory department, which had lodged in part of the main college, moved into its new home. After the
war, the western gable containing the chapel and the rooms above it was added to complete
the free-standing building with its distinctive red roof which, for the next 80 years, was to
house boys under the age of 14.

The first house master of this relocated prep unit was Fr Basil Mawson, who was brought
back from the mission at Warrington to undertake the task. For 18 years, his responsibility
was to lead the original idea through to maturity. He was a man of whom many stories were

Fr Anselm Bolton.

Gilling Castle, looking east.

69

told, perhaps because he was something of a martinet. Most relate to incidents from his schooldays, when he was an outstanding athlete who excelled in both football and cricket. It was remembered of him at his death that he was 'in every respect a leader, with a strong sense of duty and responsibility'.

The building into which Fr Mawson moved the preparatory school had been designed to house 60 boys with ease. It has perhaps never been Ampleforth's most attractive building; in the 1950s Fr Paul Nevill wrote that, 'Though the internal plan was good, the elevation was poor and unattractive and the stone, though durable, was ugly'. Unfortunately, it quickly proved to be too modest in size. The preparatory school was intended to take boys from as young as eight through to their entry into the college at 13, and space soon ran out. So, just a few years after apparently solving the problem of a preparatory school, the search for a new site started again, this time with the intention of dividing the preparatory education into two groups, the older boys remaining in the Junior House, the younger going elsewhere. More options were considered and in February 1921 a proposal to buy Grimston Manor near Gilling was put on the agenda for the Chapter. But before the end of the decade a dramatic development had made this quite unnecessary.

The Castle

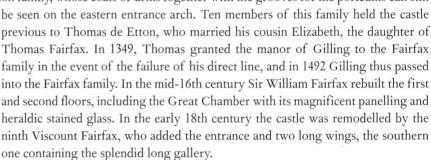

The establishment of the Community at Ampleforth was derived from the history of Gilling Castle and its owners, the Fairfax family. Gilling is an extraordinary house; its basement today is still the ground floor of the original tower house built in the mid-14th century by the de Etton family, whose coats of arms together with the grooves for the portcullis can still

Above and below:
The Long Gallery of Gilling Castle, c.1928, before its removal to the Bowes Museum.

be seen on the eastern entrance arch. Ten members of this family held the castle previous to Thomas de Etton, who married his cousin Elizabeth, the daughter of Thomas Fairfax. In 1349, Thomas granted the manor of Gilling to the Fairfax family in the event of the failure of his direct line, and in 1492 Gilling thus passed into the Fairfax family. In the mid-16th century Sir William Fairfax rebuilt the first and second floors, including the Great Chamber with its magnificent panelling and heraldic stained glass. In the early 18th century the castle was remodelled by the ninth Viscount Fairfax, who added the entrance and two long wings, the southern one containing the splendid long gallery.

It was Anne Fairfax, the daughter and only surviving child of the ninth Viscount, who built Ampleforth Lodge for her chaplain Fr Anselm Bolton to retire to after her death, when she knew that Gilling was to pass to non-Catholic cousins. She died in 1793, and there he lived until the small and dispirited band of monks came to settle there in 1802. In the 19th century the Fairfax line dwindled, and in 1895 the whole Gilling estate passed into other hands.

In 1929, just as the Community at Ampleforth was looking for another new prep school, the Castle, but not its contents, was sold to a firm of housebreakers in Northallerton. A chance had come for the Abbey Community to complete the circle by buying the castle whose owners had originally enabled them to come to Ampleforth.

So it seemed to the Abbot. In 1929 it was proposed to the Chapter that Ample-forth purchase Gilling Castle. This idea was rejected, throwing the whole future of preparatory education into doubt. It seems that two reasons lay behind this rare defeat of an Abbot's proposal. In the first place, some in the Community were worried that the purchase of the large estate attached to the Castle would be a burden. There were also concerns expressed by some that the school was growing too fast, and that it was absorbing too many members of the Community at the expense of other works. On purely numerical grounds, they were right – more and more monks were working in the school, and in the following year, the Community relinquished two of its parishes in Wales, Dowlais and Merthyr Tydfil. But Abbot Matthews was not convinced – indeed, in the December of 1929 he summoned an extraordinary Chapter to reconsider the issue, and this time the decision went his way.

In the new year, Fr Bede Turner and the architect Giles Gilbert Scott began feverish work to make the necessary alterations and additions to the building. Such was their success that in September 1930 the lower part of the prep school moved in to the Castle, still under the care of Fr Basil Mawson. The older group of boys, aged 12 and 13, remained on the north side of the valley, and the preparatory school built just a few years earlier was renamed the Junior House. This was placed in the care of Fr Illtyd Williams. This system endured the test of time. It worked without a break for 43 years until a change of policy in 1974 when both schools began offering preparatory education up to 13 years.

The castle into which the younger boys moved must have seemed like a palace to them. Certainly the Ampleforth Community had acquired, at relatively modest cost, a building of unique architectural merit. But it was not quite as glorious as it had once been. As part of the sale in 1929, the two finest internal features of the Fairfax castle – the Gallery and the panelling of the Great Chamber and its glass – had been sold as separate units. The latter had been bought by an American newspaper magnate, William Randolph Hearst, who wanted to use it to panel the castle that he had recently bought in Wales. His agents were combing the country at the time for suitable ornaments for what was to be a perfect medieval castle, and eventually they acquired 20 panelled rooms waiting for the dream to come true.

In the meantime, the Great Chamber was restored as well as was possible. A cheque for £300 was sent by Hearst's agents to cover the cost of replastering, just in time for the boys to move in. A few years later in 1936, Robert Thompson was commissioned to create new panelling, which he did with all the care he lavished on everything he made. It cost just £147.

Hearst's dream of his Welsh castle never came true. A few years later, his grand plans had led to the accumulation of debt, and the panelling remained in store, apparently forgotten. After his death in 1951, the unopened packing cases were discovered in a warehouse near London and sold to an antique dealer. This was brought to the attention of Abbot Herbert Byrne, who, realising that the Community's reserves could not alone achieve the purchase, and urged on by Fr James Forbes, opened a subscription list to raise money for the restoration of the panelling to its original home. Significantly, the first donation came from Robert Thompson, who gave the Abbot £100 on condition that he had the unique opportunity to work with 16th century wood.

Others had ideas about the panelling as well. Various local public bodies expressed an interest, and so did Billy Butlin, who apparently wanted it to line the billiard room at his holiday camp at Filey. In the event, Abbot Herbert defeated Billy Butlin and the panelling returned to Gilling, with Robert Thompson putting it back in its original home. He wrote to Fr James Forbes in 1952, 'What a relief to hear that it is all settled and the panelling is coming back to its own home'. Alongside the panelling came the stained glass, and this too was

Gilling Castle, the Great Chamber, *water colour by Fr Maurus Powell c.1935.*

restored as carefully as possible. The result was the re-creation of the Elizabethan Great Chamber as first conceived by Sir William Fairfax, which must rank as one of the most outstanding school refectories in the world.

Life in the Preparatory School

For the boys in the prep school at Gilling, their daily experience was shaped by the monks who shared their life. For the first four years of the new school's existence, Fr Basil Mawson continued as Headmaster. He was remembered by the boys as formal and brisk in manner, perhaps because so much needed to be done in creating a preparatory school out of Gilling Castle. Although Scott and Bede Turner had done a great deal of work, it seems that, when the new school moved in, many of the practical details of the arrangements of the castle were left in the hands of the Headmaster. He was succeeded by the man who had been his assistant, Fr Maurus Powell. For 14 years he led the Gilling Community, assisted at different times by Fr Henry King, Fr Anthony Spiller, Fr Bede Burge, Fr Christopher Topping and others. In 1948, Fr Maurus was succeeded as headmaster by Fr Hilary Barton, who after 17 years was followed by Fr William Price.

The early reminiscences of Gilling in this period are full of stories of Fr Maurus Powell, who clearly exercised a huge influence over the boys. He was a man of many talents, including art, handicraft and the care of birds. He was also an outstanding teacher of Latin. One of the most enduring memories of life in the preparatory school was his aviary, which contained a remarkable collection of brightly coloured and interesting birds for the boys to watch. It seems that the idea of having such an attraction was suggested to Powell by some Scottish friends of his, who provided him with several golden Amherst pheasants. Other

Gilling Castle, the Great Chamber, *water colour by Edwin Dolby, 1875.*

The Junior School dining in the Great Chamber, 2000.

birds were later added to this collection, although the golden pheasants were always the prize attraction, and made such an impression on some of the boys that in later years they remembered them as golden eagles. A visit to the aviary was a treat which pre-dated the move to Gilling – it had originally been set up at the western end of the junior house, but it moved with Fr Maurus Powell. In later years, the aviary was reduced to a single parrot, whose cage was discreetly covered during classes.

This was one of the many ways he found of entertaining boys outside class. He sometimes did sketches for them, and spent much time teaching them to use chisels and other tools, neatly engraving the name of one boy on his wooden set square using a gas heated red-hot writing point. In the evenings, he would read to them, choosing especially the novels of John Buchan. There were of course occasions when he had to be serious – one boy remembers being severely corrected on the occasion that he was found to be mending a model aeroplane on a Sunday. But the overriding impression is of a man who gave the junior boys a great deal, as expressed in these words written by Fr Bernard Boyan: "Fr Maurus' outstanding quality was his humanity. He was deservedly popular and seemed to have the knack of developing the interests of each boy."

Among the other activities enjoyed by boys in the prep school, both before and after the move to Gilling, one keenly remembered is the showing of films. The prep school did not have a projector of its own, so in the 1920s film shows were rare and involved setting up a temporary projector which had to be hand cranked at two revolutions per second for up to 15 minutes per reel. This highly skilled operation was the particular gift of Fr Hugh de Normanville, the founding housemaster of St Bede's, who presided over the showing of films until the arrival of a projection box later in the 1920s. Thereafter, Fr Maurus Powell chose the 16mm films for the boys, occasionally simulating a breakdown in the projection equipment when an unsuitable scene began.

When cinema was not available, magic lantern shows were a popular entertainment. The subjects were educational in nature and included introductions to the passion plays of Oberammergau and the monasteries of Monte Cassino and Subiaco. There were also evenings devoted to slides on different European cities, although more than one old boy now speculates that these were illustrated by the same single set of pictures. Others remember his art lectures in the Gallery on Sunday evenings.

Among the outdoor activities of the prep school, a favourite seems to have been the scouts, run by Fr Ignatius Miller and Miss Marshall. Later, cubbing also took place on half-holidays, with different years occupying various parts of the Gilling Woods. Sport took place on most afternoons, and here the significant change took place before 1921, when the junior boys abandoned soccer in favour of rugby. It is remembered how Fr Sebastian Lambert came over to initiate the boys in the new sport, 'using the blackboard and chalk to instruct us how to play this extraordinary game with 15 boys and a funny ball'. Until 1950, most of the sport for Gilling boys took place in the valley rather than at the Castle.

Fr Peter Utley, Housemaster, Junior House, 1940–48, and Commanding Officer of the Combined Cadet Force, 1940–68.

There were very few outings for the younger boys, a fact that seems surprising to the modern reader, especially considering the length of terms and the absence of any mid-term break. This gave particular importance to Fosse Day, when the whole of the prep school walked to a local reservoir where they enjoyed a communal picnic. The nearby farm did well out of this, charging one penny for a glass of milk and two pence for a hard-boiled egg. By the 1940s, the venue had moved to Sleightholmdale. On occasions such as these, the weekly allowance of pocket money was raised from the usual sixpence to a whole shilling. On normal Sundays, when there was no outing, boys could spend this money at the tuck shop run by the matron, although most reminiscences suggest that the food at Gilling was rather good, rabbit pie being a particular favourite. Fr Basil Mawson had a particular way of dealing with the very insistent demands for second helpings of pudding, allowing such a treat only to the victors of a competitive recitation of a limerick.

During the Second World War some curious changes took place in the daily experience of life for the boys. The main drive down near what is now the golf course was closed and became the site of a prisoner-of-war camp for Italian soldiers. During their enforced residence at Gilling, they refaced the front of the castle and cut down all the chapel chairs to the size appropriate to small boys.

The Junior House

At the age of 11, boys moved from Gilling to the Junior House, presided over until 1936 by Fr Illtyd Williams. He was a man of many talents, skilful at every sort of game, extending even to the playing of cards. After 1936, when he suffered a breakdown in health, he went

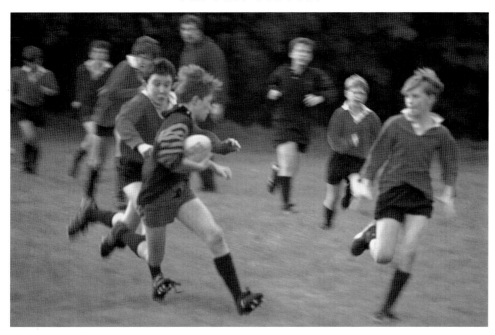

Rugby at Gilling.

on a recuperative voyage to South Africa and back, and it was rumoured in the Community that he recouped all his expenses by playing and winning at bridge and poker on board.

The Junior House was different in important respects to Gilling. Under its longest-serving housemaster, Fr Peter Utley, who presided over it from 1940 to 1968, the boys were given tremendous freedom and independence. Fr Peter himself was a powerful influence, and his death, immediately after retiring, was a shock to all. A long line of monks assisted him in the work of teaching and caring for the younger boys, who had the great advantage of being taught mostly by staff from the Upper School. As a result, the quality of education offered in these years was very high.

An important change in the structure in Ampleforth's prep schools took place in 1974. There had been difficulties with the split prep-school education from the first. For example, Gilling, without senior boys, was not able to compete in sport with other prep schools. At the same time, the two-year experience of the Junior House was perhaps too transient for boys to really feel a sense of belonging. So the decision was taken to give Gilling its own top two years, enabling boys to stay there until they moved to the Upper School. At the same time, the Junior House was expanded into a three-year group, beginning at the age of 11. The hope was that this would prove attractive to parents whose children had been educated up to that age in primary school.

It has perhaps been in the area of prep-school education more than anywhere else that the modern period has seen significant change in the pattern of parental choice. Decline in national prep-school numbers began in the late 1970s, and in the early 1990s it became increasingly difficult to justify the maintenance of two separate prep schools which were, in effect, competing with each other. So in 1993 the decision was taken to create a new school at the Gilling Castle site, Ampleforth College Junior School, which combined the existing boys from both Gilling and the Junior House. At the time of writing, a further change is being put into effect, with the merger of 'ACJS' with St Martin's School to create St Martin's, Ampleforth.

10

The Community and its Works 1939 to the Present

It is natural for a history of any British institution to pause and restart in 1939. The onset of the Second World War brought with it many changes, and the monastic community, school and parishes were each in their own way affected by it. But for another reason, the same year marks a break in the story we have been telling. On Good Friday morning, having presided at Mass on the previous day, Abbot Edmund Matthews died after 15 years in office. As the second Abbot of Ampleforth, he had presided over many changes and developments, above all the growth of the school described in an earlier chapter. His experience of Ampleforth stretched back to the 19th century, through the heady years of Prior Burge and the foundation of a house in Oxford. His successor, elected under the shadow of the impending conflict with Germany, was to lead the Community for the next 24 years, up to the eve of the changes inaugurated by the second Vatican Council.

Abbot Herbert Byrne
Fr Dominic Milroy

In the dark years of the mid-20th century – the Second World War and its aftermath – the zenith years of Winston Churchill coincided with, and were echoed by, those of Paul Nevill and Herbert Byrne. Hardship generates a hunger for leadership, a readiness to be inspired by great men capable of saying memorable things. Fr Paul and Abbot Herbert were very different in temperament and vision. Fr Paul was expansive, optimistic, grandiloquent and, in the full Florentine sense, magnificent. Abbot Herbert was cautious, inclined to pessimism, ironic and self-deprecatory. What they had in common was a remarkable capacity to create, as it were from nothing, sayings which were so characteristic of the particular genius of each that they could never be anticipated before being uttered but, once uttered, had a certain unforgettable obviousness. Each was, in his own way, both inimitable and highly open to attempts at imitation, and both

Ampleforth 2000.

Abbot Herbert Byrne,
1939–63, by James Gunn.

generated, throughout the school and the monastery, an insatiable taste for affectionate mimicry.

'HKB', as he was usually known, was not only temperamentally opposite to 'Posh' Paul. He was also more than somewhat suspicious of Fr Paul's expansionist vision of Ampleforth, and made it his business, as Abbot, to promote a fairly dry and austere monastic spirituality which was largely indifferent to what was happening in the school. There can be no doubt, however, that Abbot Herbert was profoundly influenced by everything that Paul Nevill's educational philosophy represented – its humanity, its liberalism, its 'Englishness' – and that his greatness as Abbot lay in a very special gift of 'osmosis' which enabled him to grow into the full reality of modern Ampleforth without compromising his own vision of what a Benedictine monastery should be.

This was only one of the several personal tensions and paradoxes of HKB. 'To live is to change, and to be perfect is to have changed often'. HKB was the embodiment of Newman's remark. He was, in particular and at every level, a remarkably 'educated' man: from a lonely childhood as the son of a Merseyside Irish tanner to a Classics degree at Oxford which equipped him to make jokes in Ciceronian Latin at the Abbots Congress in Rome; from a severe and even puritanical early formation to the radiantly genial serenity of his abbatial style and of his later sunset years. It was because he was very aware of his instinctive severity that he was able, so successfully, to moderate it as he grew into the particular and 'liberal' ethos of the Matthews-Nevill version of English Benedictinism.

HKB was intensely aware of what he owed to the English Benedictine Congregation. He not only came to embody its style; he was also hugely perceptive and eloquent in expressing it. By temperament a lover of monastic silence (he loved the Latin word *quies*), he was above all a wonderful chooser of words, both formally in his gracefully Edwardian discourses and informally in his almost Wildean sallies. His pessimistic caution became increasingly transfigured by a kindly irony in which he took evident delight and which gave delight to his hearers even when it had a hard edge.

When a monk remarked that he was reading a book called *Difficulties in Mental Prayer*, HKB simply commented, 'It must be a very long book.' When the guest master introduced him to a guest with the comment, 'Guy is a bit outspoken, he always says what he thinks,' HKB replied, 'Ah, very good. I hope he has nice thoughts.' On appointing a monk to look after the school theatre, he added a final comment as the monk was leaving the room: 'And remember, taking part in theatrical productions does boys nothing but harm.' It was the quizzical, over-the-spectacles smile which made his mastery of the art of deflation so invariably unwounding. When a novice was bold and patronising enough to thank him for one of his conferences, HKB replied, 'Ah – thank you, Brother, but (pause) be warned; Ampleforth monks do not normally thank each other.' But behind his reiterated insistence on the difficulties of the monastic vocation ('It is above all a matter of going on . . . and on . . . and on') his monks could readily perceive the radiant example of his own hard-earned peace of soul.

Hard-earned it no doubt was. By his own admission, the tension between his instinctive severity and his need for ordinary human affection had not, in his early years, been an easy one. The resolution of this tension had been achieved, at different levels, by his fidelity to monastic charity and to the ordinary channels of grace, by the increasingly confident affection shown to him by his brethren, and by his assiduous cultivation, in himself and in others, of an all-pervasive sense of humour. He used irony, understatement and sheer wit as servants of an immensely civilised courtesy, which created spaces of equality without diminishing his authority as Abbot. By a strange and happy paradox this very austere man became, for his Community, not only a living example of 'what sort of man the Abbot should be', but also a mysterious and refreshing channel of laughter. He once surprised a novice indulging in an abbatial imitation in the cloister; he said nothing, smiled in mock reproof over his spectacles, and walked away, chuckling. The same chuckle lay just below the surface when another novice had the misfortune to drop a load of crockery in the cloister just as HKB was passing. 'The bottom of the cardboard box gave way, Father Abbot,' blurted the novice. After an inimitable pause, HKB replied, 'It would have been more perfect, Brother, not to offer an excuse.' Without a smile, this would have been a fairly classical (and humbling) monastic response; but HKB's twinkle was just (only just) evident enough to transform it into a courteous family joke. He had, above all, the gift of using irony as a means of building happiness.

The shadows of war

In the immediate aftermath of the declaration of war with Germany, the *Ampleforth Journal* was able to record that 'whatever the effect of the outbreak might have been on individuals, we must admit with gratitude that it has affected Ampleforth as an institution but little so far'. If this was true in 1940, it was forgotten by 1941, by which time all of Ampleforth's works had been changed by the impact of conflict.

Left to right: Frs Paul, George, and Stephen.

Inset: Fr George Forbes, MC, Chaplain to the Guards 1940–45.

Fr Edmund Fitzsimons.

The first change was permission given to three members of the Community to enlist as chaplains to the forces. From the parishes, Fr Gabriel McNally became an army chaplain and was present with the troops during the final retreat to St Malo after the battle at Dunkirk. Fr Aelred Perring left his parish ministry to work with the Royal Air Force in the Middle East and elsewhere. From among the monks working in the school came Fr George Forbes, whose example and heroism as a chaplain earned him the distinction of the Military Cross. Part of the citation states that: 'He was an inspiration to the whole battalion, and I am not skilled enough with a pen adequately to describe his conduct.' He saw service mostly in Italy, where he had the extraordinary experience of watching the allied destruction of Monte Cassino, the monastery and shrine of St Benedict.

The effects of the war on the parishes varied greatly, according to the vagaries of the wartime bombing campaigns. In all of the parishes, the experience of young men leaving for war and not returning presented its own challenges to the monks serving on the missions, but no monk had a more direct experience of war in the parishes than Fr Edmund Fitzsimons. Working at St Anne's in Liverpool in 1941, he was caught up in the blitz of that city. A few days after the event, he wrote to Abbot Byrne to describe the experience reflecting that 'as far as I am concerned it is very simple – I was the subject of a first-class miracle.' He had been in Overbury Street helping the police and air raid wardens, when a land mine exploded by a boys' school just alongside him. He wrote:

> They say you cannot pray on these occasions – I did. I made a good, if rapid, act of contrition – I thought I was finished. I knew I had missed the blast by a fraction but I just lay there waiting for something to fall on me – nothing did – although bits of iron and concrete fell all round me.

When he got to his feet he realised that he was the only living being in the area. The policeman to whom he had spoken only minutes before, rescue workers and others were dead, and he helped to dig their remains out from the ruins.

Ampleforth itself was never bombed. The railway line was attacked once and an incendiary bomb started a fire in the chapel at Gilling which was put out by the prompt action of Fr Bede Burge. One can only imagine that these were accidental. Bombers in their hundreds certainly flew over, the German squadrons apparently using the abbey church as a marker in their journey towards Middlesbrough, Newcastle, Glasgow and Liverpool. In the later years, the sky above the valley was filled on most evenings by allied bombers on their way to Germany.

The threat from the air was real enough, and a system of air raid precautions was quickly put in place. The shelter for boys and monks alike was in the basement area of the monastery library, as indeed it had been during the Zeppelin raid threat in the First World War. The monastic choir was blacked out completely, and Ampleforth was one of the few places where Christmas Midnight Mass was celebrated. One year, the liturgy was broadcast by the BBC into occupied Europe.

By virtue of its location, Ampleforth was able to offer immediate shelter to others fleeing from war. In the autumn term of 1939, Bootham School was evacuated from York and occupied the Junior House. The boys who would normally have lived there were given a new home in the old infirmary, while boys who would have joined the Junior School that year stayed on at Gilling. In the summer term of 1940, Avisford School arrived, apparently at

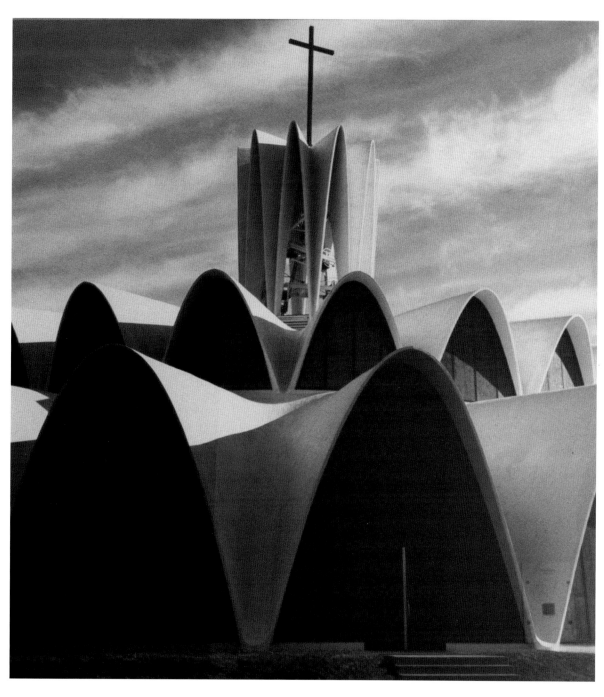

The Abbey Church, 1962, at St Louis, Missouri, founded from Ampleforth, 1955.

only two days' notice. The school infirmary, the gymnasium and even the indoor swimming pool underneath the theatre were converted to house them, the *Journal* noting laconically that 'the swimming bath was made a little more accommodating by being emptied and boarded over'. At the end of what must have been a remarkably cramped term, Bootham returned to York, and Avisford were thereafter accommodated for the rest of war in the Junior House.

There were also prisoner-of-war camps in the area; there were Italian prisoners at Oswaldkirk and Gilling and Germans at Thirkleby and Northallerton. A number of monks were involved as chaplains, notably Fr Barnabas Sandeman, and extra Mass centres were set up to serve evacuated Catholics. There was also a Polish hostel in Oswaldkirk, set up for Polish boys in the school.

Many changes affected the life of the school. Blackout precautions, ration books and all the other consequences of war had their impact, as indeed did the increasing death toll amongst old Amplefordians. By the end of the war 121 old boys had died, and over 1,000 had served in the forces. The *Ampleforth Journal* reverted to the practice it had adopted during the First World War, namely including in each issue a roll of honour, a list of those wounded and missing, and some short obituaries of those who had died. In 1943, it was calculated that 172 old boys were serving in the Royal Navy, 537 in the army and 127 in the Royal Air Force, figures that grew in 1944 as the D-Day campaign began.

The reminiscences of the boys in the school during that period highlight a number of unusual activities to which the needs of war subjected them. The first was the creation of the 'land army', led by Fr Oswald Vanheems, part of the national 'Dig for Victory' campaign. The original members of this group came from the Agricultural Society, and it has been estimated that, during the years of war, they lifted more than 22 tons of potatoes and 61,000 head of other roots. During the holidays from school, this work continued with a group of boys staying at Gilling Castle to work on the land there. Each of the school houses, indeed, created their own vegetable plots, and it was perhaps a sign of things to come that St Edward's House was particularly noted for the quality of its crop.

There was always the chance that some boys might take the risk of wartime too lightly. Perhaps for this reason, a special visitor arrived in 1941 – a caravan which parked on the square under the supervision of the local police constable. Each boy was asked to attend this with his gas mask, and inside the caravan they got some sense of what the effects of a gas attack might be like. We can presume that, after this exercise, the carrying of respirators became much easier to remember.

Inevitably all aspects of school life were affected by war. There was no formal Exhibition during these years, simply a prize-giving without a play or concert. The call to serve in the forces meant that ground staff were reduced to a minimum and few cricket matches were played except against local army units.

For the monastery, the question that presented itself most urgently in the early years was whether or not to continue receiving men for the noviciate. From 1939 to 1941 this remained open, and the monks themselves were not faced with conscription because of the exemption granted to ministers of religion. The system did not always work, however, and one professed junior, Br Leonard Jackson, was swept up into the forces in 1939. This awkward situation was resolved when Br Leonard telephoned a War Office official and impersonated the Abbot, thereby procuring the exemption that was his due. After 1941, only one person was accepted into the noviciate. The result was that, when the noviciate was re-opened in 1946, there were

Br Leonard, 'telephoned a War Office official and impersonated the Abbot.'

Abbot Basil Hume 1963–76 by Derek Clarke, c.1972.

ten candidates to be clothed. The noviciates of the following years remained large. Many of these novices had much experience of active service in all three Services.

Confidence and change

The war ended slowly, at least as far as rationing was concerned. One little example, which can serve for many others, is the fact that potatoes continued to be grown in the quadrangle until 1949. The wider Community of Ampleforth had suffered greatly, as witnessed by the roll of honour which forms the centrepiece of the northern end of the school library, the Memorial Library. The names of those who died were carved on Hoptonwood stone by the then librarian, Fr Patrick Barry.

But the early 1950s saw a renewed period of expansion, which took monks of Ampleforth in the apparently unlikely direction of the United States of America. Two foundations had already been made there from the English Congregation and in 1951 Fr Aelred Graham of Ampleforth had been appointed Prior of Portsmouth, Rhode Island. In 1954, a group of residents of St Louis, Missouri, visited Ampleforth and expressed to Abbot Herbert their concerns regarding Catholic education in the city. After a careful investigation by Fr Richard Wright and Fr Robert Coverdale, and Community discussion, the Chapter gave permission in January 1955 for a foundation to be made in the city for the explicit purpose of establishing a secondary school. Three monks were sent initially to make this foundation, Fr Columba Cary-Elwes as Prior, Fr Luke Rigby and Fr Timothy Horner and a fourth, Fr Ian Petit, soon joined them.

Fr Patrick Barry, Headmaster 1964–79.

It took some time for the new monastery to establish itself, but in 1957 the first novices were sent to Ampleforth to begin their formation. This proved very hard for the young Americans concerned – the change in culture was perhaps greater than anyone had perceived, and the sheer distance between the novices and their home proved an enormous obstacle to overcome. Other monks from Ampleforth were sent out to support the Community in its work, and in 1967 Fr Columba returned to England, to be replaced as Prior by Fr Luke Rigby. When St Louis became an independent house in 1973, Fr Luke became its first ruling Prior, and when in 1989 it was raised to the status of an abbey, he was elected as first Abbot of the Community.

For the monastic community as a whole, this was a period of expansion. The post-war noviciates were large, creating the sense of optimism which underpinned the St Louis foundation. In 1953, Fr Basil Hume and Fr Martin Haigh established the Ampleforth pilgrimage to Lourdes, building on the much older tradition of more *ad hoc* groups of monks and boys visiting that shrine. School numbers also grew steadily, so new school houses were founded, as described in an earlier chapter.

The most striking change in the school came with the death of Fr Paul Nevill in 1954. For 30 years he had been its guiding hand, and he died quite literally at his desk, his breviary in front of him. The choice of a successor to a man who had become so important in the story of Ampleforth, and indeed in the wider world of education, was inevitably a difficult one. The Abbot's choice fell on Fr William Price.

A sense of the task that Fr William faced can be gained even now by spending a moment in front of Derek Clark's massive portrait of Fr Paul in the central building. The searching gaze of the eyes and perhaps above all the mastery of Headmaster over the school behind him demanded much of any successor, and it was perhaps to Fr Williams' advantage that he

Cardinal Basil *by Andrew Festing 1991, gift of John Gibbs.*

Abbot Basil was appointed Archbishop of Westminster and later Cardinal in 1976.

Abbott Ambrose Griffiths, 1976–84, by Stanley Roseman.

was so different in background and outlook. After the First World War he had gone to Oxford, where he was introduced to St Benet's Hall by Br Christopher Williams. During his undergraduate years he explored Catholicism, and was received in the church at Ampleforth. After graduating he became a lawyer, working for British American Tobacco in Shanghai before joining the monastery in October 1933. After just two years, he began the work of teaching and administration that was to occupy the rest of his life. Over 35 years he taught a series of subjects in the monastery, modern history in the school, boxing and, in 1951, became housemaster of St Wilfrid's in succession to Fr Columba Cary-Elwes. After just three years in this post, he became Headmaster.

He inevitably adopted a different approach to his predecessor. He was never hands-on, keeping a benevolent eye upon the whole operation and showing interest in the big issues rather than details of administrative paperwork. He presided over the school in a less personal way, perhaps reflecting something of his shy nature. There is a story of a prospective parent who on his first visit recalled that he had not been able to meet the Headmaster, but had been shown round instead by a delightful monk called Fr William. For ten years he provided the school with what it needed at the time, and what he himself described as a 'bridge passage'. In 1964 he was given a break of a year, during which he went to Portugal and visited the monks of St Louis, before returning to Ampleforth to become Headmaster of Gilling. He died, still in office as Fr Paul had been, in January 1971.

The ten years during which Fr William was headmaster saw the beginning of changes to the pattern of education and the formation of the young which were to gather speed and intensity in the following decade. In place of Fr William, Fr Patrick Barry took on the challenge of adapting Ampleforth College to the new spirit of the 1960s. This involved fundamental changes to the shape of the life of the school. Corporal punishment was quietly abandoned, and many of the facets of the 1960s revolution had to be encountered with moderation and care. Perhaps the most notable feature of this period as regards the academic life of the school was the growth in the numbers and responsibilities of the lay teaching staff. This development has continued up to the present day

The changes in education in the 1960s were mirrored by the changes that affected the whole of the Catholic church in the aftermath of the second Vatican Council. There is a striking concurrence between the beginning of this time of transformation and the abbatial election of April 1963, when, after 24 years in office, Abbot Byrne was replaced by a young housemaster aged only 40, Basil Hume. For the first time in the history of Ampleforth, an Abbot had retired rather than died in office, and it is a mark of the quality of Abbot Herbert as a monk that he accepted this change of life and new role with such obvious willingness. For the future, a man was needed whose vision could take the Community over the troubled years ahead, and the greatest testament to Abbot Basil's tenure of office is the relative ease with which the Ampleforth Community, both at home and on the parishes, faced the many daunting issues of the age.

With the advantage of hindsight, we may note two enduring changes from the many that were raised at this time. The first, which we will touch upon later, is the change from an entirely Latin to a predominantly English liturgy. The second lasting change concerns the number of parishes attached to Ampleforth, and the number of monks serving them. In fact, decisions to relinquish control of parishes and hand them over to the care of the local diocese go back at least to the 1920s, and a number of parishes had to be relinquished in the 1950s. However, from the mid-1960s this changed from being an exceptional event to a pattern,

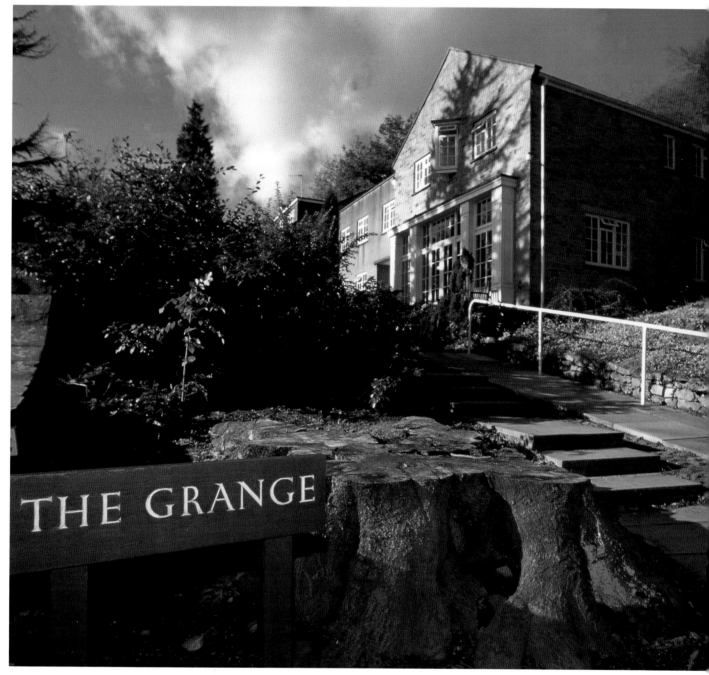

The Grange – guest house since 1972.

although it never had behind it any desire to abandon the tradition of missionary work in parishes altogether. Inevitably, there was pain involved in relinquishing each and every parish, especially those with a long tradition of association with Ampleforth such as St Peter's Liverpool and three of the parishes in Warrington. It was frequently hard on parishioners and monks alike to make the change. At the time of writing, Ampleforth monks continue to serve 14 parishes, a number which has remained relatively constant since the mid-1980s. This still represents a very significant part of the work of the Community.

*Abbot Patrick Barry.
1984–97*

Abbot Basil was appointed Archbishop of Westminster and later Cardinal in 1976, and in his place the Community elected Fr Ambrose Griffiths. Formerly senior Science master and then Procurator, it was his task to continue the process of renewal that the Council had called for. He led the Community for eight years, after which he served as parish priest of Leyland before his appointment as Bishop of Hexham and Newcastle.

It is not possible to assess the history of this post-Conciliar period with detachment – we are just too close to it. However, it is possible to note three developments over these decades which are significant in themselves but also point to wider changes in the life of the Church.

The first of these grew out of the Council's concern for ecumenism. Abbot Basil established a forum for interaction among local clergy of different denominations, the Abbot's Group. Then in 1968, the decision was taken to establish a house for boys from Orthodox Christian communities at Ampleforth. The site chosen was the former hostel for refugee Polish children in Oswaldkirk, and in 1968 St Simeon's was opened under the care of Fr Vladimir Rodzianco. This enabled Orthodox boys to be educated at Ampleforth and it was also hoped that it would become a centre for other ecumenical activities.

A second change was the diversification of work at the Abbey. In 1971, the Community Chapter supported a plan, spearheaded by Fr Kieran Corcoran, to develop the Grange, previously the farm manager's cottage, into a residential centre for parish groups, students and conferences. Alongside the development of Redcar Farm as a youth hostel, this marked a notable broadening of the work of the Community as well as enabling growing numbers of guests to attend the monastic liturgy.

A third change flowed from the desire of some in the Community to seek a more simple way of life wherein the priority of prayer was very evident. Many years of discussion of how this might be effected led to the investigation of a number of options, including the possibility of developing the parish of Rixton as a site for a new foundation. In 1977, permission was given for an experimental house of prayer and hospitality to be established at Ince Blundell, which has continued as Ince Benet.

Central Building.

In 1984 the Community elected Fr Patrick Barry as the sixth Abbot of Ampleforth. After many years as Housemaster of St Wilfrid's and Headmaster, he had also experienced the wider work of the Community in its parishes before his election. He led the Community until 1997, when Fr Timothy Wright was elected to succeed him. Abbot Timothy's reflections on the ongoing story of the Community form the Foreword of this book.

Buildings

At Ampleforth itself the most obvious visible change since the 1960s has come from the constant building work in support of both school and monastery. Following from the building of Aumit House, the early 1970s saw an enormous process of expansion according to the plan put together by the architects Arup Associates. The construction of the east wing

St Dunstan's House, built 1972–73.

of the school, originally to contain the staff Common Room, Modern Languages and Geography departments was matched by the building of Nevill House in 1972–73 to contain St Oswald's and St Dunstan's.

Both these building projects were necessitated by the increasing structural weakness of the Old House at the centre of the campus. Fr Anselm Bolton's original house had seen many uses, and by the early 1970s it was showing many signs of strain. The withdrawal of residential accommodation for boys did not mean the abandonment of the building, which remained in use for offices, music classrooms and the monastic refectory well into the 1980s. But it made the likelihood of the replacement of the Old House with a new central building all the more likely, a plan which finally came to fruition in 1988. Before then, two substantive new facilities were created for the school in the St Alban Centre (1975) and the Sunley Design and Technology Centre, built in 1982. The redevelopment of the central area was made possible through the generosity of donors to the Appeal, which included among its achievements the building of the new monastery Infirmary (a temporary refectory during the period of rebuilding in the centre) and the new music school attached to the old gymnasium. Finally, the new Central Building, designed by Desmond Williams, was opened to act as the Old House had done, as a bridge between monastery and school. In this Appeal as in all the developments of the century, Ampleforth is indebted to its many generous lay benefactors.

The Dalai Lama and Abbot Patrick Barry, 1984.

The 1990s has seen further building work, made necessary by the continuing pressure to ensure the quality of school facilities. In 1996, a decision to centralise catering services in the school led to a substantial remodelling of the Upper Building, one of Scott's listed buildings, by the architect Martin Stancliffe. In the year 2000, the new Business Studies, Economics and Science building was opened through the generosity of Sir Anthony Bamford, and in 2001 the Community celebrated the memory of Cardinal Basil Hume by naming a new double house below the School Infirmary after him, into which moved St Wilfrid's and St Cuthbert's.

Monastery, Church and World

One of the most striking features of Ampleforth since the 1960s has been the growing interaction with the wider Church and world. It would of course be quite wrong to caricature Ampleforth before this date as insular or inward looking. A man like Anselm Burge, with his breadth of vision and interests, gives the lie to any such impression. Nevertheless, the 1970s saw a notable renewal of this interaction, of which one clear sign was the elevation in 1976 of Abbot Basil Hume to be Archbishop of Westminster and Cardinal. In the previous year, Fr Dominic Milroy, housemaster of St Wilfrid's, had been appointed Prior of Saint Anselmo in Rome, the international Benedictine house of studies and headquarters of the Abbot Primate of the worldwide Benedictine Confederation. In 1983, Fr Placid Spearritt, then Prior, was appointed Administrator of the monastery of New Norcia in Western Australia, of which Community he became Abbot in 1997. During the 1980s links were forged with a movement in Chile, the Manquehue Apostolic Movement. Such new movements have been characteristic of the church since the Vatican Council, and the Manquehue Movement had as its particular focus the education of the young in schools inspired by the Rule of St Benedict and the monastic tradition of Lectio Divina. Both old Amplefordians and monks have become closely involved with this over the years, and in the 1990s the Manquehue Movement was formally associated with the Ampleforth Community.

Initiatives by Abbot Patrick have led to a number of new foundations in recent years, taking monks of Ampleforth into new forms of pastoral and apostolic activity. In 1986 the Community made a foundation in York, an experiment in urban monasticism combined with the running of a diocesan pastoral centre called St Bede's. In 1994, this Community made way for a new foundation at Osmotherly, where the monastic day was combined with the care of the parish and of the medieval shrine of Our Lady of Mount Grace.

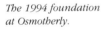

The 1994 foundation at Osmotherly.

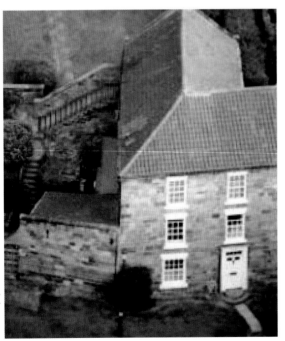

In 1996, the most far-reaching foundation was established in Zimbabwe, with the opening of the monastery of Christ the Word. Unlike the earlier foundation at St Louis, this did not have a specific focus on education or parish work, but rather sought in the regular monastic life to become a centre for prayer and renewal in that country. The task facing this new foundation was understood as threefold: first, to build a monastic community which could act as a witness in that culture; second, to develop means of earning their living; and third, to provide a place of hospitality. As was written in 1996:

> The church in Zimbabwe is young and active and many of the young, along with those not so young, are in need of a place apart. They need to be encouraged to go deeper in their relationship with God in prayer, in reading the scriptures and in understanding their faith. To join in the life of prayer and work of a stable community could do a lot to encourage others who live often in very poor and difficult situations.

A third foundation marks a new phase in the development of Ampleforth's parish apostolate. In 1999 an old convent adjacent to the parish church at Brownedge was opened as St Benedict's monastery, from which monks serve the neighbouring parishes in the South Ribble valley.

The 1990s has also seen a growth in a traditional monastic work, that of hospitality. Since the merger of Junior House and Gilling, the old Junior House building (renamed Alban Roe House), has become a centre for youth groups and others visiting Ampleforth. The number of guests overall has also increased. An annual programme of retreats and courses, combined with the welcoming of groups of all sorts in the school holidays, allowed as many as 14,000 guests to come to Ampleforth in the year 2000.

Top: *monastery buildings, and* above: *monks, of Christ The Word established at Monte Cassino, Zimbabwe by Ampleforth in 1996.*

The Abbey Church

At the heart of Ampleforth, both physically and more importantly in terms of identity, lies the Abbey Church. This ever-imposing edifice never fails to surprise new visitors, first of all because of its date. Completed in the autumn of 1961, it seems an unlikely architectural expression of that tumultuous decade. When that has passed, a second surprise follows, namely the austere interior, the lack of decoration that can prompt some visitors to ask with apparent innocence, 'Is this a Catholic Church?' After that comes a final surprise, the sense of vastness and of silence contained within its three great domes. It would be wrong to pass by this opportunity to celebrate this building, which for the last 40 years has presided over Ampleforth.

The building of the Church

At the opening of the new Abbey Church on 8 September 1961, the sermon was preached by the Archbishop of Liverpool, the future Cardinal John Heenan. It comprised an extensive meditation on the history of monasticism and its churches, based upon the perception that the ideal of the monastery as a rural idyll, untouched by the world, had never been true except in the imaginations of the romantics. For Heenan, it was entirely proper to the Benedictine spirit that Ampleforth should have waited until 1961 before completing its church:

> It is to the great credit of the Ampleforth monks that the building of this splendid Abbey Church was their last and not their first concern.

What he is pointing towards in this remark is the fact that the new Abbey Church was constructed in response to a need rather than in pursuit of an ideal. Fr Edward Corbould, writing in 1961, observed that 'a building is not a beauty in a shell, nor utility in a shed, but an answer to a particular problem', and for the Ampleforth Community and its school, that problem was space. By the beginning of the 20th century, the church built by Joseph Hansom in 1857 was becoming too small, and as early as 1905 animated discussions had taken place within the Community about a possible replacement. In April 1919 an approach was made to Giles Gilbert Scott, the young architect who had astonished his contemporaries by winning

Left: *Demolition of the Hansom church, 1957.*

Top: *The Hansom church, south side, c.1940.*

Above: *The Giles Gilbert Scott church, from the same viewpoint, 2000.*

the competion to build the magnificent Anglican cathedral at Liverpool. Following the brief he had been given, he produced a plan, and a contract was signed in 1922 to begin the building work. The first part of his design was completed two years later, consisting of the choir, high altar and the four crypt chapels beneath it. This was constructed alongside the old church, so beyond the high altar, which was some twelve feet west of its present position, the new choir merged with the old church, all of which became the nave. This was hardly Scott's plan, but the money had run out.

It was to be another six years before discussions on the next phase even began. During the 1930s a number of plans were produced, but at the outbreak of the Second World War no decisions had been taken. In 1952 the process started again, and a final set of plans was accepted in 1954. Money was still short, and the building of the main body of the Abbey Church was made possible only through the generosity of donors to the Appeal run by Fr James Forbes.

The first step in this new phase was to take down the Hansom church. This was started early in 1957, and the first stones for the new Abbey Church were laid in that April. Throughout this period, and until the completion of the building programme, the school liturgy took place in the celebrated 'Tin Church', a steel-framed shed covered with asbestos sheets, which was erected on the lawn west of the school library. It was, quite properly, called St Laurence's, and it formed the setting for a series of monastic professions and ordinations as well as the annual liturgical cycle. For a short time, indeed, it proved necessary for the Community's conventual Mass to be celebrated in the school library.

The new Abbey Church followed the outline that had been established by Scott in the 1920s although his original vision had even considered five domes, one each over the north and south transept. The first of its great domes was built above the choir, and the second

Facing page: *St Laurence*

91

The Abbey Church under construction.

Facing page:
The Abbey Church.

The 'Tin' Church.

two covered the sanctuary and then the nave. Throughout the planning and even the building process, there were continual concerns expressed over the need to accommodate the rapidly expanding school, but Scott always resisted the pressure to extend the nave too far. Writing in 1948, he expressed his view that an overlong church would cramp the school buildings to the east, create a church in which much of the congregation was too far from the altar, and above all distort the whole vista of the campus. He argued that:

> The external grouping of the church with the surrounding buildings would be better with a more or less symmetrical arrangement around a central tower . . . This gives a balanced centrepiece to the whole group of buildings forming the south front.

The final building remained faithful to this vision of a symmetrical focal point for Ampleforth. The transepts to north and south were enlarged, and the great high altar arch was moved twelve feet eastwards on specially constructed rails so that it could be seen from the sides. The result is a church of remarkable solidity, that appears to have been here for centuries.

Scott's design was indeed influenced by much earlier models. In particular, he had been impressed by a group of Romanesque churches in the Aquitaine area of France, constructed in austere fortified towns like Perigeux, Cahors and Angouleme. He believed that something of their nobility and simplicity was appropriate for the edge of the North Yorkshire moors, and he was right. The central square tower, rising to 37 metres (122 feet) , is perhaps especially characteristic of Scott's kind of building. He clearly rejected the kind of grand Gothic spire that Bernard Smith had originally conceived for his ambitious rebuilding of the whole of Ampleforth in the 1890s.

There are some differences of architectural finish which mark the earlier stage of the building from the later sanctuary and nave. The choir area was constructed using blue Hornton stone which, by the 1950s was simply too expensive to use. Thus the latter part of the church is more simple, with large interior areas of unadorned plaster. The eyes of the visitor are drawn inexorably upwards, with so little to distract them at ground level, towards the great domes, each of which is 32 feet in diameter. The building thus expresses something essential about monastic prayer, that nothing should distract the ears of the heart from listening and responding to the Word of God.

The consecration of the church in 1961 was a great occasion. The western side of the high altar had already been

dedicated to St Edward the Confessor in 1924, but on 6th September 23 prelates, led by the Archbishop of Liverpool, consecrated the altars in the new church. The nave side of the high altar was dedicated to St Laurence, the patron of the Abbey. After the consecration, the first Mass was celebrated by Abbot Herbert Byrne, who four months earlier had marked the golden jubilee of his priestly ordination by an open-air Mass on the lawn in front of the monastery. Two days later the newly consecrated church was formally opened by Cardinal Godfrey, who was spared the awkwardness of the actual consecration of the nave, for which process Archbishop Heenan had had to be raised up on a specially constructed scaffolding. It is said that, on approaching the scaffolding, he confessed to being deeply afraid of heights, such that the master of ceremonies, the future Abbot and Bishop Ambrose Griffiths, had to support his arm throughout.

The anchor of identity

Although the Abbey Church was built to answer a very particular and practical need, it was always conceived as being more than utilitarian. It is, like all great churches, a proclamation of identity, a statement by the Community of St Laurence of its history and vocation. Three features in particular, perhaps, capture something of this.

In the first place there is the high altar and its arch. Scott regarded this centrepiece, completed in 1925 and the gift of Francis and Audrey Gibbons, as among his masterpieces. On the choir side of the arch are depicted four saints, all of whom are closely related to the Abbey of Westminster: St Peter its patron, the monastic reformer St Dunstan, St Wulsin or Wulstan of Westminster, and St Edward the Confessor, the king who refounded the Abbey and to whom the choir side altar is dedicated. On the nave side, the saints proclaim a different message. Two of them, St Francis of Assisi and St Ethelreda or Audrey, are an expression of the Community's gratitude to the donors of the arch. St Laurence, patron of the Abbey, is depicted holding the bag of money which was his particular responsibility as a deacon in Rome. It is a reminder of the famous story told of Laurence that, when forced by his persecutors to hand over the wealth of the Church, he pointed to the crowds of the poor believers and said, 'Here is the wealth of the Church.' On the north side, parallel to St Laurence, is the most unlikely figure of all, St Anne, mother of Our Lady, holding her child in her arms. This is associated with the feast of the Presentation of Mary on 21 November, the day on which Sigebert Buckley, the last survivor of medieval English monasticism, had ensured the continuity of the English Benedictine tradition and, by virtue of that, its inheritance by the Community of St Laurence.

A different sort of identity is expressed in the westernmost side chapel of the upper church, dedicated to Benet (St Benedict). The altar screen shows Benedict blessing his first two disciples, Sts Maurus and Placid. Below this is the Byland Abbey altar stone, given to the Community in 1870. It is clearly marked with five consecration crosses, and in its centre is the box which would once have contained a relic. This altar, along with the alabaster Byland Trinity on its left, acts as a particular symbol of the continuity of monastic life in this valley.

The alabaster Byland Trinity.

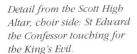

Detail from the Scott High Altar, choir side: St Edward the Confessor touching for the King's Evil.

A third part of the church which remains in the memory of everybody who encounters it is rarely seen. The abbey tower contains just two bells, of which the smaller, named Giles, was originally cast in 1658. It had rung from Newcastle Cathedral and Langley Castle in Northumberland before it came to the Abbey as the gift of T. Bates. It weighs about half a ton, whereas the larger bell weighs nearly 5 tons. It is named as Gregory John in memory of its donors John Kassapian and Gregory Fattorini, and can be heard for many miles around. Blessed in July 1960, it was specially cast for the church, and the dedication inscription says something important about what the Abbey is for:

> Let the sound of these bells be united with the prayers of monks and the voices of boys: I Gregory John call the faithful to praise God and to the prayer of supplication.

*'Gregory John':
4.5 tonnes, A flat.*

The Mouseman

No account of the Abbey Church would be complete without mention of the work of Robert Thompson, who worked alongside Scott in the first phase of the construction of the Abbey Church, and whose oak choir stalls and other furniture are one of the beauties of the building. Thompson's enduring legacy to Ampleforth was, of course, far greater than in the church alone, but this is a suitable point to record his involvement in the great programmes of building and restoration of the first half of the 20th century.

Robert Thompson was born in the village of Kilburn in 1876, and after a brief and unhappy time in industry he followed his father as a joiner and carpenter. He worked on anything that came his way, including the restoration of the tower of Gilling parish church, on which he made the single gargoyle that sticks out on the north side. In May 1919 he met Fr Paul Nevill, then working on the parish of Ampleforth village, who commissioned him to produce the village crucifix. This was the beginning of a friendship between the two men that lasted more than 30 years, and through it he became involved first in work in the church and then in the school. He constructed the Abbot's stall in 1928, famously carving the arms of the Abbey on a single piece of wood, and he then did the stalls to either side. In 1925 he constructed the first of the carrels in the School Library, before turning to the Upper Library and then in 1950 to the Memorial Library at the north end. At the same time he was building his characteristic 'Ampleforth chairs', not only for the library but also for the school houses. His final piece of work for Ampleforth was the memorial door to Fr Paul in the library, completed in 1955. All of his work is marked, of course, by his characteristic signature of the mouse, an expression in wood of his favourite motto, 'industry in quiet places'.

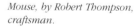

Mouse, by Robert Thompson, craftsman.

It was through his work for Ampleforth and the contacts made by the Community that Thompson's reputation as an ecclesiastical craftsman spread. He worked on furniture for several of the Ampleforth parishes, including Bamber Bridge and Workington. He was also asked to produce the screens and choir stalls at Fort Augustus Abbey. Such was the quality of his work that, having completed the carving of stalls for a chantry at York Minster, the Dean declared that his work 'will stand as a witness to posterity of our own generation's creative . . . ability'.

The south Choir.

St Laurence relic.

The Church since its completion

There have been few visible changes to the Abbey since its completion and consecration. The reforms of the Second Vatican Council, coming so soon after its opening, led to the introduction of new altars in the choir and in the nave, and most significantly transformed the use of the crypt. With its 24 chapels, this had been designed for the celebration of Mass by each individual priest and server every day. In September 1965, the first concelebrated Mass took place, and since then the practice of 'private masses' has declined. The crypt remains as a place of prayer and is used for occasional quiet or group liturgies.

These visible changes to the fabric of the church are of course merely the most obvious sign of the far deeper transformation in the liturgical life of the Ampleforth Community inaugurated by the Council. To some extent, this spirit of reform had been anticipated in the 1950s by the restoration of the Easter Triduum by Pope Pius XII, first celebrated at Ampleforth in 1953. The Easter vigil of that year was remembered as 'an impressive and moving climax' to this series of celebrations, which took place with the whole school present. One member of the monastic community wrote that:

> Even if one has some regrets for the change, it is hard not to think that the merits of the new ceremony will establish it as a loved and traditional rite.

The liturgical reforms introduced from the mid-1960s were more far reaching and controversial. The most obvious change involved the translation of the Divine Office from Latin into English, which began with Compline and then extended to all the other Hours except for Vespers. The decision to retain this office in Latin, using the ancient plainchant, was entirely in keeping with the Council's vision for a liturgy in which the beauty of the Latin could exist alongside a new English text. For the English, a whole new set of psalm tones and antiphons were composed by members of the Community.

The relationship between the liturgical life of the school and the abbey church had begun to change from well before the Council. The six outer houses were built with their own house chapels for daily Mass, while the four inner houses joined together each morning in the abbey church. During the 1960s, obligatory daily Mass became increasingly counter-productive, and regular fortnightly or monthly confession, once the practice for the whole school, was replaced by a more flexible pattern again focused on the house. As a result, the inner houses created their own house chapels, and the abbey church became associated above all with the celebration of Mass on Sundays and other high solemnities. In this regard, the most far-reaching change involved the intro-

96

duction of the Schola Cantorum, which was greatly developed after 1970 by David Bowman with the support of the Headmaster, Fr Patrick Barry. In both the Sunday Mass and through the Schola Mass on Friday, the quality of this choir has become widely admired, leading to numerous overseas tours and recordings.

In fact, the earliest recording of music from Ampleforth pre-dates the foundation of the Schola by almost 40 years. In 1929, the *Yorkshire Post* reported that 12 monks had travelled from Ampleforth to London 'for the purpose of recording ancient plain song music on the gramophone'. This was the first recording of sacred music made by any religious community in the country, and was the inspiration of Fr Bernard McElligott, then Choirmaster and the founder of the Society of St Gregory for the study and practice of music in the liturgy. The first sound broadcast from Ampleforth was at Christmas midnight Mass in 1940, and the first televised liturgy took place in the newly completed Abbey church in October 1961. From the early 1980s the Schola began making their own recordings, and in 1994 the monastic community produced its first compact disc, *Vision of Peace*.

The desire to share in the experience of the choir at Ampleforth has not been limited to recordings. Since the 1970s, guests have been permitted to sit in the choir, a decision which at that time was a very radical innovation. It still remains unusual, even in continental monasteries, for guests to be welcomed to share so closely in monastic prayer. Fed by the growing numbers attending the retreats in the Grange, the presence of such guests marks one of the most notable changes in the use of the church since the Council.

Walker organ, 1961.

A unique moment in the liturgical year occurs every Easter, when the Community opens its doors to large numbers of guests who stay at Ampleforth, using even the school dormitories and sharing in the liturgy of the Triduum. Originally conceived as a retreat for old boys, this grew steadily under successive guest masters, and in 2001, 397 guests were registered for this retreat, with as many as 500 attending the liturgies themselves.

The campus of Ampleforth has changed much over the four decades since the completion of the Abbey church. There has been extensive development to the east, and the uses of some of the buildings to its west is changing, yet Scott's original vision of a confident and unambiguous heart for the worshipping community remains a powerful statement of what Ampleforth is truly about. It is an enduring testimony to vision, and a clear statement in stone of the belief that inspired St Benedict 1500 years ago, that in the life of a monk 'nothing should be preferred to the work of God'.

Fr Laurence Bevenot
Fr Adrian Convery

Ludovic Bevenot became a monk of Ampleforth in 1919 taking the monastic name of Laurence. He had come to the school from Mount St Mary's in 1914 and finished as Head Monitor. He was a gifted pianist, organist and musician although, apart from instrumental lessons, he never had any formal musical training; the climate at Ampleforth in those days was suspicious of the arts and especially of music. After his noviciate and philosophical studies he was sent to St Benet's Hall in Oxford to read mathematics. He delighted to recall with gratitude how Fr Dominic Willson gave up smoking in order to pay his termly subscription to the University Music Club. He completed his theological studies at Ampleforth and was ordained a priest in 1928, having already succeeded Fr Bernard McElligott as Choirmaster and Head of Music in the School in 1927. Most of his time, however, was devoted to teaching mathematics.

He was not a natural schoolmaster, and he found the unremitting task of correcting books a burden. His classes could be unconventional – a prep devoted to writing a definition of a wheelbarrow, exercises on taking moments of a ten-ton cheese. An end-of-term report states succinctly: 'His wits evaporated at the sight of the exam paper'. He soldiered on stoically for 25 years, but his heart was in music, and music was regarded as a spare time activity to be fitted in when and where possible. Nor was it expected to cost money, so that he had to spend countless hours making music stands for the school orchestra and arranging and copying music – special parts for boys of limited ability which he designated HBLO (hard bits left out) or, sometimes, for the more gifted HBPI (hard bits put in).

In 1929 he had been one of the co-founders of the Society of St Gregory under Fr Bernard McElligott, and he attended every annual summer school until 1990. For many years he taught plainsong accompaniment and one recalls some memorable moments: one nun he named Sister Consecutiva from her propensity for writing consecutive octaves and fifths, and he once chided a would-be accompanist as he reached the climax of the Gloria, 'My dear boy, you can't leave God the

Father suspended on a first inversion.' He was also a regular contributor to the pages of *Music and Liturgy*, writing articles with quirky titles such as 'The Quilisma, its habits and haunts'.

In the early 1940s he was greatly influenced by his friendship with Susi Jeans and developed a love for early music and the baroque organ. He became interested, too, in keyboard temperament and was responsible for the development of an organ, now in Alison House, Edinburgh, built by Harrison's of Durham and designed by Dr A McClure, with a normal keyboard but nineteen notes to each octave. For a year this was in the Memorial Chapel, its case decorated by a Yorkshire rose carved by himself, and he used it to accompany the monastic plainsong and later demonstrated it at the Edinburgh Festival. About this time he was a moving force behind the revival of the Hovingham Festival together with Fr Austin Rennick and Lady Read.

Stone carving became a major interest from the early 1940s after what he described as a memorable meeting with Arthur Pollen. Besides lettering many of the headstones in the monks' cemetery, he also designed and carved the very lovely stone housing for the reliquary to St Laurence in the north aisle of the Abbey Church, the memorial to Michael Fenwick in the Crypt, and a crucifix in the Big Passage.

Fr Laurence Benevot.

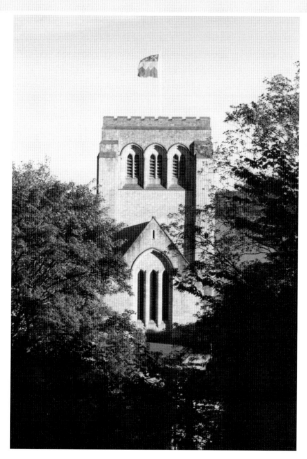

The Abbey church, north side.

99

12

Work and Play

It is impossible to do anything more than offer glimpses of the daily life of the boys in the school in the 20th century. Each of the areas that are contained in this chapter could be the subject of a study in itself, and much of the detail of the religious, academic, sporting and social life of the school has perforce been omitted. In some areas there is just too much to say, whereas elsewhere the evidence is patchy. Much depends upon individual reminiscences, each of which has a particular slant and betrays the interest of the person writing it. Nevertheless, what follows is a series of studies in miniature, which taken as a whole say something about the boys at work and at play over much of the 20th century.

The work of God

For much of the early part of the century, the school day began with the celebration of Mass, often at 7.30 am or earlier. The boys were woken up either by a bell or by a monitor, but some would have to rise earlier in order to be available to serve the private Masses of the monastic community. In many of the recollections of this period, it is this intimate experience of the liturgy, with just one priest and his server, which dominates the religious life remembered by old Amplefordians. There was something special about it, even though very practical concerns also intruded. There was certainly a desire, for example, to serve the Mass of a priest known for his speed rather than those distinguished by the slowness of their devotion. Yet behind this sort of anxiety, it is possible to see something of the impact of an experience, which placed a boy in such proximity to the action of the Mass. For some, indeed, it proved decisive in fostering a sense of vocation to the monastic life. Serving at Mass could also have its lighter side. In the 1920s, Fr Dunstan Pozzi used to say Mass every Sunday at the home of the Sykes family at Sledmere, and he was in the habit of taking a server with him. Not only did the lucky boy have the experience of being driven in a two-seater Morris Cowley (or even driving it himself!) but there was also a good breakfast and a chance to see round the house itself. Boys especially remembered seeing the cellars and the Turkish bath.

Sunday was of course a special day. There were two Masses, a Communion Mass and the High Mass, and the whole school also attended Vespers on Sunday and Benediction on

Sunday and Saturday nights. The Mass included a sermon, and a number of reminiscences reflect on the pleasure that could be gained from the first sermons of the newly ordained, whose words could be taken to pieces later by this remarkable critical audience.

A particular concern of some was to avoid being in the church choir, led from early in the century by Fr Bernard McElligott. Choir members lost all their free time on Tuesdays and Fridays to practice, and the only reward was the choir day out on the Feast of St Cecilia in November. Plenty of advice was available on how to avoid being selected, although membership could have its advantages, especially for the lower voices. Fr Bernard was said to have remarked more than once that 'boys could sing on an empty stomach but tenors needed a good dinner'.

In 1927 the choir was taken over by Br Laurence Bevenot, a demanding task not only because of the reputation of his predecessor but also because the choir included both boys and monks. It was remembered that his approach was different in at least two important respects – he reduced the amount of general joviality during practices, and more seriously (for the boys at least) he banned one of their favourite pieces, a Vittoria Mass.

Throughout the early part of the century, the religious life of the boys was utterly instinctive. Ampleforth College was entirely Catholic, and the outlook was formed by the same fixed points of religious devotion as in the whole Catholic world of the period: the Mass, the rosary, regular confession and retreats. The whole school had a silent retreat twice a year for most of this period, one in October and the other during Holy Week. Outside retreat givers were usually invited, and many of the boys remember the words of Monsignor Ronald Knox, whose 1939 retreat coincided with the sudden death of Abbot Matthews. Perhaps these words, written of Ampleforth in the 1920s, express something of the simplicity and depth of this faith:

The House system.

101

Development of each boy's Catholic faith and practice was in the air we breathed. The general awareness of boys was not concerned with future scholarship or wealth . . . It was understood that what matters most was the Catholic Church's teaching (not one item of it was ever questioned), of loving God and our neighbour – combined, if and when opportunities arose with responsible leadership.

Near the athletics track, 1943.

Matters academic

For all this, education mattered very much, and it was the consistent policy of the period to enhance the academic quality of the school. In the first Exhibition after the death of Fr Paul Nevill in 1954, the boys and their parents were reminded that his principal concern had been to ensure the maintenance of a high level of scholarship, and the Exhibition brochures of the years of his headmastership speak eloquently of the number of boys obtaining places in Oxford and Cambridge.

The primary element in the curriculum was the study of the classics. As late as the 1950s, a really bright boy might be able to go through the school doing little else, and other subjects certainly knew they were in second place. Among the modern languages, French was taught, but others only as and when the need arose. During the 1920s, a German class for four boys was included in the timetable, although all of them had previous experience of the language, and one pair of brothers included in the set had been told to do German by their parents 'because the family view was that we were going to have a war against the Germans'. The change in this approach, and the development of new subjects in the curriculum such as Design and Business Studies, is one of the most notable features of the modern curriculum. This is reflected in the buildings of the last two decades.

For those who were taught, it is often the teacher rather than the subject that stayed in their memory. Perhaps for this reason, there are a large number of stories which speak of the teaching of Fr Placid Dolan, who taught mathematics in the school for 37 years. It is remembered how, on one occasion, he wanted to demonstrate the difference between static and sliding friction, and to do so he placed a glass of water on a piece of paper on the edge of the desk. Unfortunately, he had failed properly to dry the bottom of the glass after filling it, so when he pulled the paper away, the glass leapt into the air, showering both monk and boys with water. It seems that he was able to live up to his name even in this crisis, and remained remarkably calm while the class went wild with laughter.

Officers of the OTC, 1942.

After prayers in the big passage and the first classes, the boys had their morning break, when the school (in two halves) did P.T. on the Square and Ball Place. In the 1920s, this was the opportunity for delivering the post, which was done in an unusual fashion. Many of the reminiscences of this period recall how the monitors flicked letters out of a library window for those waiting on the square. In the general scramble to retrieve them, it is amazing that damage was not done. What happened to letters belonging to those who were not waiting for them, or indeed to any parcels, no one seems to know.

Break time was also the time for a particular Ampleforth form of punishment known as the penance walk. This could be imposed by a master or a monitor for a variety of small offences, and involved a solitary and silent walk up and down in front of the old house. An impression of the sort of offence that might merit this was given when Fr Edmund Matthews, at this time Headmaster, spoke to the school at the beginning of one term about a particular offence which he had noticed. His concern was the prevalence of catapults among the boys, for he noted that the face of the clock above the New College 'had five indentations and three perforations'.

The inventive quality of misdemeanours has been a constant feature of school life. One such occurred in 1947, when the monks noticed that an unusual additional ornament had been placed on the

Members of the 1st XI, 1943.

theatre gable. A boy or a group of boys unknown had climbed the building overnight, and left a chamber pot at its peak. The novices were dispatched to remove the offending item, but it proved a demanding task to get the ladder high enough to achieve this. In the midst of their struggles, Fr Robert Coverdale emerged from the bottom of the Big Passage, calmly removed a .22 rifle from under his habit and shot the chamber pot to pieces. Both novices and boys were undoubtedly impressed, so much so that a few days later, a further chamber pot was found in the same place. This time, no novices were summoned, but Fr Robert opened fire again. This time, however, the bullet ricoched off the chamber pot, which remained stubbornly intact – the boys had had the foresight to replace the porcelain pot with one made of tin.

School life

One reason why boys might have aimed missiles at the clock was that many of them had to sleep, or try to sleep, immediately beneath it. In almost every generation of reminiscences, there is a smattering of expressions of deep loathing for the clock and its chime, which as it marks the quarter hour has always proved capable of keeping certain people awake. This apart, life in the long, cubicled dormitories is remembered by many with affection, although one boy has never forgotten his sense of shame when, apparently by mistake, he was asked to sleep in a part of the room known for obvious reasons as 'Stinkers' alley'. Pictures were allowed in the individual cubicles, but their subject matter had to be strictly religious. The Sacred Heart, pictures of Saints and other holy images were encouraged, but one boy was seriously reprimanded by Fr Hugh de Normanville when he found a picture of Ginger Rogers.

Many boys from the pre-war period remember the twice-weekly bath very clearly. This great occasion was presided over by the lay brother Peter Woolley, whose particular job it was to ensure that no one boy got more than his allotted ration of hot water. In fact, many of the memories of this period concern the lay brothers, perhaps because they were an object of interest, being different from the monks who taught and led the school and its liturgy. Apart from Br Peter, who was regarded as a disciplinarian because of his control of the hot tap, there was the more amiable Br George, who would sometimes rescue a spare piece of apple pie to put in the desk of a boy who was feeling particularly low. Br Ernest and Br

Matthew between them were responsible for cleaning and mending the shoes of the boys and were remembered with fondness and affection. Br Matthew continued to clean the shoes of St Oswald's house into the 1950s.

The cleanliness of the boys' shoes was part of a general emphasis on their appearance. For most of the first quarter of the century, the boys wore suits on weekdays and special suits with a pinstripe on Sundays. Each boy also had a hat, but this was only worn on journeys at the beginning and end of term, so that the hats spent most of their lives sitting in trunks. When the house system was first introduced in the 1920s, boys wore house badges on their blazers, known as Bluers, a practice which died out in the 1970s.

The memory of the food served to the boys in this early period is surprisingly positive. Ironically, most people seem to have preferred the menu offered on Friday rather than on any other day, because Friday meant fish, and potato pie. This was the speciality of the cook, Bert Natter, and it was marred only occasionally by the presence in the pie of a suicidal cockroach. In 1910, the system whereby certain boys' parents paid for 'extras' was abandoned, and from this point everybody had bacon for breakfast and bread and jam at tea, previously the privilege of the few. At one time, draught beer was also available every day for the sixth form.

For their medical needs, the school was served from the twenties by the unambiguously functional Infirmary on the road to the east of the school. It has done more than 70 years of service, though changes to the facilities within began quite soon after its completion. From 1930 it had a basic operating theatre, which was never used, and an x-ray machine was also installed. This not only enabled the broken bones and other injuries of the boys to be diagnosed quickly, but also proved to be of service to the local community.

Rarely has the Infirmary proved too small to meet the needs of the school. The occasional epidemic of flu has always presented problems, of which the first and most serious was in the 1920s. On very rare occasions, boys were accommodated in the monastic infirmary, although this was usually only in cases where, on medical advice, boys were required to spend the holidays recuperating at Ampleforth. One boy remembers spending Christmas with the Community, and the room next door to his in the infirmary was made over to his father, who travelled up to be with him at this time. Both were looked after by the legendary monastic infirmarian, Fr Cyril Corr, who presided over the infirmary for over 30 years from 1897.

Pursuits, serious and otherwise

With the expansion of the school in the early 20th century there came a new emphasis upon clubs and societies for a range of activities. Some were notably serious in orientation – in 1915, Fr Hugh de Normanville founded the Scientific Club, which was still running many years later and, at the Exhibition, the biennial Scientific Conversazione was held, in which members of this and the Natural History Society discussed their research interests. Similarly serious in outlook were the debating societies, both for the upper and lower school. The records of these debates provide precious insights into the mentality of the school at different periods, and much can be learnt both from the subjects discussed and from the final vote. Thus in 1940, the senior debating society discussed the motion that Neville Chamberlain had created, by his actions, an entirely unnecessary conflict. This was resoundingly defeated. In the same year, the boys debated whether the life offered in the countryside was better than that offered in the towns and cities of Britain, and this time the ayes had the upper hand, winning the vote by 21 to 3. Two years later, the most serious debate concerned whether England could any longer be regarded as a Christian country, and the view of the senior debaters was that it could not, an interesting forerunner to the modern discussion of the same question. Politics was always an interest, such that in 1954 the most lively debate of the year was over whether Britain should revive an Imperialist policy. After some hours of discussion, the result was a tie at 26 votes for and against.

Other academic clubs rose and fell according to the interests of the boys and the enthusiasms of the Community. In 1957, the Archaeological Society was revived after a gap of more than three decades, while the Forum was a society devoted to the study of things literary and intellectual. Lovers of the history of art were for a time served by the Leonardo Society, while the Historical Bench remained constant, although numerous annual reports lamented the small numbers who attended. For a time, Fr Columba Cary-Elwes presided over a society called Les Voyageurs, devoted to enjoying tales of travel to foreign lands. In later years he himself could have told many such stories.

Other societies with more relaxed aims also appear in records of the school. There were at different times clubs devoted to the enjoyment of railways, the making of model aeroplanes, the watching of birds, and Highland reels. Indeed, a strong tradition of dancing endured into the modern period, and a display of country dancing was a feature of the annual Exhibition until the 1960s. One year, the boys even danced competitively in the Albert Hall.

As was noted in an earlier chapter, the 19th century school at Ampleforth seems to have been remarkable for the range and intellectual calibre of its internal publications. In 1935, an ambitious new scheme gave birth to the longest-running school magazine, the *Ampleforth News*, the idea of Robert Anne and Hugh Fraser. Throughout its history, it has taken a somewhat irreverent look at the goings-on of school and monastery, famously portraying Ampleforth monks and boys repelling German invaders parachuting into the valley on a wartime cover, the work of John Ryan. *The News* has lasted with only few breaks for some 65 years, far longer than any of its rivals. More significant was *The Wind and the Rain* (N. Braybrooke and M. Allmand).

One of the most remarkable achievements in the history of school publications at Ampleforth must be the 1947 volume *The Ampleforth Country*, written by a group of boys with the guidance of Fr Columba. This went through four editions, being revised and

Fr Cyril Corr, *by Fr Sylvester Fryer.*

Piano practice at Gilling.

printed most recently in 1966. The authors of the original edition expressed their aim in the following words:

> Why should a group of boys set to work to produce this little guide? The explanation is that Ampleforth stands in a countryside which illustrates . . . the whole sweep of English history. A pamphlet appeared to be needed for the benefit of the school, and it seemed simplest for a group of members of the sixth form to expand slightly a series of notes which they had compiled. The compilers, if indeed they can aspire to that dignified name, can at best plead they had imitated the Jackdaw of Rheims. They have pilfered what interested them, went to see for themselves, and have enjoyed themselves in the process.

The resulting volume remains a delight to read, as well as being a treasure trove of interesting information and anecdotes.

Fr Sylvester Fryer, self portrait.

The arts

The beginning of the 20th century saw a change in the shape of the arts at Ampleforth. From 1861, the school theatre had been located in the Big Study, and this was used for concerts and plays as well as the characteristic Ampleforth operetta. This always had its awkward side, so when, early in 1908, the Community was offered £2,000 towards the creation of a permanent theatre for the college, there was much enthusiasm. The building to the south of the study block was completed in time for the Exhibition of 1911, when the Mystery play the *Nativity of Our Lord* by Monsignor Robert Hugh Benson was performed. The play itself was only three years old, and the whole experience was regarded as highly satisfactory. At the next Exhibition it was noted that:

> Perhaps for the first time in the Ampleforth history, the audience was able to sit through the performance without feeling cabined, cribbed, or confined for want of room.

Another important change took place in 1916 when Fr Stephen Marwood and Fr John Maddox took over the running of the theatre, beginning a long history of 'Marwood-Maddox' productions. They were succeeded by Fr James Forbes and Fr Robert Coverdale, then by Fr Kevin Mason and Fr Leonard Jackson, and then by Fr Dominic Milroy. In 1923, electric lighting was installed, and in 1924 the school received its first visiting drama company, which performed Twelfth Night to a full house. A Dramatic Society had come into being by this point, and the Green Room became steadily more adventurous in its use of both stage and lighting. In 1931, *Journey's End* was the first play wholly produced by boys. This was to be the first of many such ventures, enabling the distinctive double strand of Ampleforth's theatre since the Second World War, with large-scale and often lavishly produced plays alongside simple but powerful productions put on by the boys themselves. The tradition of house theatre competitions has similarly endured, and remain keenly contested up to the present day.

The building of the theatre also enabled the expansion of cinema. Films were shown on a regular basis from 1921, and a number of monks were closely associated with the running of the cinema box. Fr Oswald Vandeems ran it for years and later Fr Leonard Jackson. During this time it became the practice of having two showings of the film per week, using the half-holiday on Wednesday, which moved to Saturday at the end of the 1960s.

Like theatre, the tradition of visual art in the college had 19th-century roots, but its own 20th-century development. From 1858 until 1908, art was taught by a visiting master from York, William Boddy, who could count among his pupils a number of successful architects. Art also flourished within the monastic community – old Amplefordians of the 1920s and 1930s remember with fondness the sketches made of them by Fr Maurus Powell, and many parts of the monastery and school are still decorated with the paintings of Fr Raphael Williams. The Community's artistic talents moved in a different direction with the arrival of Fr Sylvester Fryer, a former Fleet Street cartoonist whose caricatures of members of the Community form one of the most tantalising archives that we have. He also taught art in the school, where he had a particular gift for any boy who showed natural talent. He was also the first art master to develop a substantial art room, with the necessary tools not only for drawing and painting but also for modelling and tooling with leather.

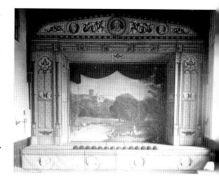

The stage in the Study, c.1905.

The teaching of art to the boys continued to develop under Fr Martin Haigh and John Bunting, under whose eyes work of very considerable merit was produced by the boys. John Bunting's particular gifts lay in drawing and working with stone, and his carvings can be seen above the west entrance to the upper building, above the cloister door to the monastery and in a number of house gardens. Fr Martin's paintings have also come increasingly into public view, culminating in an exhibition at Liverpool Anglican Cathedral in 1997.

In both art and music, one of the most significant developments in the 20th century has been the growing involvement of lay professionals in directing the work of the boys. Both a choir and an orchestra existed from the beginning of the 20th century, and a number of monks, including Fr Bernard McElligott, Fr Laurence Benevot and Fr Austin Rennick led these and other musical activities. In 1958, when Fr Austin went to St Louis, the Headmaster appointed Philip Dore as the first lay Director of music. In 1970, the appointment of David Bowman inaugurated a new era in the musical life of the school, with music becoming a fully respected academic subject. Both the choral and orchestral traditions have expanded in recent decades; the growth of the Schola as an important element in the liturgical life of the Ampleforth Community has already been described. The orchestra has grown notably in its role in the life of the school during the last 30 years, under the leadership of Simon Wright.

Various societies for the pursuit of musical interests existed from before the beginning of the century. Orchestral concerts had taken place both at Ampleforth and elsewhere from the 1880s, and there were able composers in the Community, notably Fr Egbert Turner and later Fr Laurence Benevot. A particular feature of the musical scene in the early 20th century was the annual inter-house music competition, which included the testing of the singing ability of each house in solo items, part singing and unison chorus. For most of the 1940s, it seems that St Bede's House excelled in the quality of its singing.

The outdoor life

The beginning of the modern relationship between Ampleforth and sport can be dated very precisely. In 1911 soccer was abandoned in favour of rugby, which started immediately after the school retreat with a match between two school sides. Very properly, the headmaster kicked off the first ball. A group of monks were assisted from the first by lay coaches, notably Charles Wright of Harrogate. In those early years victories were rare, except the defeat of St Peter's 150–0 in 1914, but enthusiasm for rugby seems to have existed almost from the first. One old boy speaking of the 1920s writes simply that, 'rugby football was the thing', and other winter sports were pursued only when the ground was too hard. In such circumstances, cross-country and even hockey were alternatives, but they were not taken nearly so seriously and there was little or no training. The most remarkable team in this period was that of 1921, captained by the future games master Fr Terence Wright. They won all seven of their matches, 358 points to 20 and it was found convenient to instal higher goal-posts to allow notable kicking. The whole school was expected to turn out to watch any First XV rugby match, and the next year when the new set of goalposts arrived Sedbergh christened them by beating the home side soundly. Since its inception, the annual achievements of the First XV were recorded in the *Journal*, and sport proved an important point of contact between monks and boys. Many Old Amplefordians remember the coaching given in the 1950s by Fr Basil Hume and Fr Anthony Ainscough. In 1963 John Willcox, an England full back, joined the staff and for some 30 years led teams to national prominence in school rugby, especially in the Sevens Competitions at Rosslyn Park.

There were occasional heretics. Fr Raphael Williams was remembered for holding the view that the real quality of a school was revealed not by how it played rugby but by its cricket. This was however a lone voice – in the 1920s, the lower sets for cricket did not have their own dedicated fields, and the afternoon game might begin by getting the heifers off the pitch. In this, the boys were often helped by the farm manager, Peter Paul Perry.

The golden age of cricket at Ampleforth came after the First World War and was inspired by Fr Peter Utley, a former county player for Hampshire, who led a generation of boys in the sport by the power of his own magnetic example. In the late 1950s, the increase in the size of the school made it impossible for all the boys to play cricket at once, and this spurred the development of athletics. This sport had a long history at Ampleforth, and the annual athletics meeting in the 19th century was always held on Easter Monday. This increase in numbers moved most athletics to the summer, but the house competition has stubbornly remained in the Easter Term to this day.

Other sports like swimming, boxing and tennis have played their own part in the outdoor life of the boys. The outdoor pool built alongside the cricket pavilions around 1895 could be used as long as the water temperature had reached 58°F, later 62°F, and a swimming club was founded in 1930. A little indoor pool below the theatre was used. Both were abandoned when the St Alban Centre pool became available in 1975.

1947.

2001.

Left to right: Fr Dominic, Abbot Basil, Fr Benet, Fr Patrick, Bishop McClean and the former Yorkshire and England cricketer, Len Hutton c.1973.

Peterborough Champion, 1938.

Hunt meeting at the Abbey. Fr Walter and Jack Welch.

One outdoor activity taken very seriously by the school as a whole was the Officer Training Corps, formally established in 1911. This was initially divided into two squads, of which the 'B' squad was notably inferior and only did drill. Various forms of military training, and especially shooting, were considered important in the acquisition of a Certificate A, which in the 1930s helped guarantee that, in the event of war, a boy be later commissioned as an officer. In 1940, 294 boys participated in the annual field day, and in the following year the Air Training Corps was formed. The OTC was led by monks, first Fr Edward Parker and thereafter Fr John Maddox, Fr George Forbes, Fr Peter Utley, and more recently Fr Simon Trafford and Fr Edward Corbould. Fr Peter was awarded an OBE for his services to school Cadet forces.

Of all the outdoor activities associated with Ampleforth, perhaps the most famous is the hunt. The arrival of the beagle pack is recorded in the *Ampleforth Journal* for 1916:

Hitherto the recreative activities available for the corporate enjoyment and the benefit of the school have been diverse sorts of games. Sport has not been obtainable during term except by the fishing club, which jealously restricts its numbers. We owe the removal of this deficiency to Mrs Cullinan, who with kindly perspicacity discerned our need, and with prompt munificence supplied it by the gift of a pack of beagles. We declare our gratitude for so handsome a present.

This grandiloquent paragraph, part of a wider article in which the anonymous author quotes Virgil in support of the noble pursuit of hunting, marks the beginning of a long tradition at Ampleforth. Associated especially with the history of the hunt is Fr Walter Maxwell-Stewart who, for 47 years from 1941 to 1988, was the honorary secretary of the Ampleforth College Beagles and the longest serving Hunt secretary in the whole country. His first experience of running with the hounds was just seven years after the arrival of the first pack, and in the 1931 season, when he was at the top of the school, he was the Master. Much of the prominence of the pack and its success at shows around the country has been attributed to the quality of his direction, his care for boys and hounds alike, and above all his natural and instinctive love of nature. He also cultivated assiduously the links between Ampleforth and the local farmers, whose support and enthusiasm formed such an important part of the hunt.

Scouting started in the school at about the same time as the hunt. Most of the development happened in the 1930s and then after the Second World War, with Scouts proper in the junior house and Sea Scouts and Rovers in the upper school. It was largely through the energy of Fr Paschal Harrison that all aspects of scouting developed. This latter activity involved the use of the lakes, on which many boys learnt the skills of handling boats.

The most legendary incident in the history of Ampleforth scouting took place during the Second World War, and will

Goremire Day, 'some other way'.

be forever associated with one of the largest characters in the history of the Community, Fr Jerome Lambert. During a scout camp on the Isle of Islay in 1945, Fr Jerome and his troop spotted a German submarine in a bay, and proceeded to capture it with all the determination characteristic of him in all his activities. In fact, the submarine had been captured and renamed HMS Graf by the Royal Navy in 1941, but had parted its tow in a storm. Despite this detail, the story of Fr Jerome's discovery of a German U-boat must rank as among the finest and most unlikely exploits of the Ampleforth Community and School.

There were always trips out of Ampleforth during the term. During the first half of the century there was no half term, but whole holidays, usually on Holy Days of Obligation, provided an opportunity to do something different. On one occasion, most of the school joined a special train at Gilling, had an excellent breakfast on board and proceeded to RAF Cranwell, where the boys toured the station, experienced flying and had lunch. The school returned by train, and during the journey dinner was served.

Every summer, the school and monastery were emptied of all male inhabitants, so that the buildings could be given a proper clean, and out of this need was born Gormire Day. In the 1920s, it began with a litany, after which the boys walked or found some other way of getting to Sutton Bank. There, school and monastery enjoyed a vast picnic, for which beef was carved on site and wine served to the adults. The importance of Gormire Day was clearly impressed on the minds of the boys, such that when one new and enthusiastic cricket captain proposed a practice for that day, his fellow monitors made it clear how severely they disapproved of any such suggestion. Stories of the many and varied ways in which the boys travelled to Gormire are legion, with one boy even hiring a camel from a local circus. Unsurprisingly, this got into the *Yorkshire Post*.

A chapter such as this could extend forever. There are many stories that offer all sorts of glimpses into the life of the school at different periods, and many of these stories are still going on. Each generation of boys adds its own. It is now time to return to the narrative, and to the growth of the upper school in the modern period.

Jim Fox extending the cricket fields.

13

Uncompromising Hope

The College at the End of its Second Century   by Fr Leo Chamberlain

When Fr Patrick Barry first addressed the Headmasters Conference in 1971, he used the title 'Uncompromising Hope'. The phrase is a fair summary of Ampleforth's development through the vicissitudes of two centuries, and of an enduring vision. Institutions built in stone and with a history are often regarded as having passed through their history impervious to the gales and storms of their time. Nothing could be less true; every generation's skill and effort is needed. Every Headmaster of Ampleforth is conscious of the ideals and commitment shared with his predecessors, conscious perhaps also, just sometimes, of the bright wings of the Holy Spirit over the world. We have adapted to the needs of the times, but have been uncompromising in Christian faith and hope. Always, we have aimed to support Catholic families in the education of their children. That Ampleforth now welcomes all who accept the Word of God in scripture is owed both to the opening provided by the Second Vatican Council, and to the changing perceptions especially of our neighbours in the north-east of England.

English Catholic institutions, disadvantaged in every possible way as they were re-established in their native land in the early 19th century after the centuries of exile, impecunious, socially disregarded by the Protestant establishment, knew they had no assurance of a future. There have been times in Ampleforth's past, notably during the Prior Park episode of the 1830s and before the fresh impetus of Oxford educated monks in the 1900s, when the school might have disappeared – and whether the Abbey would have survived without a work on the spot which earned revenue is a moot point. In more recent years, the new eagerness of schools (one of which expelled a boy who became a Catholic in the early years of the 20th century) to recruit Catholics, and the decision of some Catholic families to put rapid access to a boarding school above more traditional and religious considerations, posed a new problem for a school 200 miles north of London.

Yet, in another sense, the Headmaster today has to do exactly what Fr Edmund Matthews had to do: to ensure that Ampleforth can offer an education second to none, to provide something for those who share our faith, and ideals that they will want for their children. This was the fundamental reason that Fr Edmund Matthews sought to establish the house system. It was finally achieved by Fr Paul Nevill, backed by the now Abbot Edmund. In the same

Walter Shewring

search for the best in education, Fr Edmund began the employment of highly competent lay masters: Horace Perry (music) and Dick Goodman (chemistry) arrived in 1924. Fr Paul appointed many others, perhaps most notably Walter Shewring (classics), James Macmillan (mathematics) and Tom Charles Edwards (history).

The Community of the time, with whatever hesitations, supported what was proposed, and the 1930s, the time of the great economic depression, saw the building of Bolton House, the Quadrangle, the Range, the Upper Building and the creation by Robert Thompson of the College Library. It was a remarkable period, during which there was constant work to recruit pupils; the key was the absolute harmony between Abbot, Headmaster and Procurator, the courageous Fr Bede Turner. They worked as one to achieve a vision, which was, as Abbot Edmund constantly put it, to make it unnecessary and unacceptable for Catholics to send boys to non-Catholic schools.

There followed after the war further development: the Memorial Library and then the foundation of St Thomas's House. Fr William Price inherited a school with a burgeoning demand for entry, so that he oversaw the foundation of two more School Houses, St Hugh's and St John's, and both a tightening and broadening of the academic life of the school: it was

Fr William Price, Headmaster 1954–64, at Goremuir, 1945.

Schola Cantorum, *2001.*

113

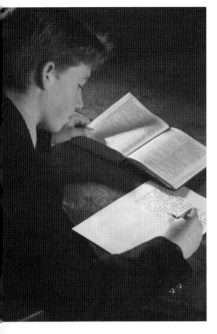

only in 1957 that Ampleforth started teaching A level English in earnest. It was all quite a programme, and it brought the establishment of Ampleforth as an academic school able to compete with its Anglican rivals, even outdoing them in point of antiquity, for in 1922 the College of Heralds recognised the Abbey as the successor of Westminster. Ampleforth was then as it is now, a school teaching well over a wide range of ability.

There was a fourth vital figure in the counsels of the time: Sir Giles Gilbert Scott. No architect can be better than his brief, but within that limitation Sir Giles was infinitely adaptable, patient and persevering in trying to give the Community what was wanted. There were many reverses and changes of decision along the way, but in the end the Abbey Church is his memorial.

In the last 40 years, development has continued. Fr Patrick Barry became Headmaster three years after Ampleforth's first appeal had achieved the completion of the Abbey Church. He was faced with acute problems over buildings. The great building effort for the school had taken place some 25 years earlier, and the need for improvement of the central teaching accommodation was obvious – significant parts of it were housed in wooden buildings already evidently inadequate. The school lacked an adequate indoor swimming pool, and had no indoor sporting facilities beyond its gymnasium. Worse, the original Ampleforth Lodge (where the first three members of the Community had joined Fr Anselm Bolton in December 1802) was in an alarming state. The optimists of the 19th Century had added a further storey to it that had proved too much for the foundations, and it had been hastily propped up in the 1940s when the dangers became apparent. So it was urgent to replace it with a new house. It was almost equally urgent to provide extra teaching rooms, and to provide better personal space for junior boys to do their preps; the old-fashioned desks of the Big Study would no longer hold the books needed by the schoolboy. Arup Associates was commissioned first to make a feasibility study, and then to design the first buildings needed to fulfil the proposed strategy. Nevill House removed St Oswald's from the centre, and provided St Dunstan's with a building so that the House was together for the first time, to the dismay of its sixth form, who had enjoyed their independent life in the rooms which were then above the refectories in the Upper Building. The East Wing provided some extra teaching rooms, and, for the next 15 years, a common room and studies for the lay staff. More wooden buildings extended the space for prep work, and space for an expanding art department. Music was provided for in the original building, now known as the Old House. Up the hill to the east rose Saint Alban Centre, a swimming pool, squash

Four generations of Goslings in one line at Ampleforth.
Left to right: *V. Gosling, 1895, G. Gosling, 1945, J. Gosling, 1973, L. and T. Gosling, 2002.*

courts and sports hall, and St Thomas's gained a new wing, leading to the closure of Romanes, which for 25 years had housed its sixth form.

These buildings were the instruments of an expanding vision of an Ampleforth education. Throughout the period, Amplefordians went to Oxford, Cambridge and increasingly to other leading universities in satisfactory numbers, to read a growing variety of subjects. Ampleforth's earlier strengths had been in the classics, history and mathematics, with excellence indeed to be found elsewhere, as in the well regarded modern languages department, but the balance of numbers and of the curriculum favoured those three subjects, just as games and country sports were seen as the healthy leisure occupations for the Ampleforth boy. The picture was never wholly unbalanced; debating flourished, the school won the Observer Mace in the 1960s, and there were always determined musicians, artists and writers, as the lists of Old Amplefordians indicate. But Fr Patrick perceived the enormous value of music in education. He saw also that here was the one possibility open to us, under a Labour government intent on dismantling links with the independent sector, of securing an entry to Ampleforth for at least some who could not afford fees. The initiative brought with it the refoundation of a Schola Cantorum, brought quickly by David Bowman and his successors to a high standard.

Simultaneously, Ampleforth's traditional disciplines, religious and secular, were under question. The student disturbances of 1968 marked the coming of an emphatic new collective identity for the young and found an echo at Ampleforth. The dismissal of what was loosely called the establishment carried for many the dismissal of religion. There was a clear need to rethink the approach to religious practice and to pastoral care. The changes in the forms of discipline were a part of the process. Corporal punishment by monitors was ended as soon as Fr Patrick became Headmaster in 1964; it was ended altogether without announcement in the early 1970s. Housemasters had lost a quick answer to nonsense, but it was not otherwise evident that good order was damaged. More important, there was a consistent effort to establish a rethought discipline; and the writing of 'lines' (the copying 40 or more

Prayers in a House Chapel.

times the principal parts of a Latin and French verb) that had been the fate of many junior boys in the past largely ceased. Yet it would be mistaken to suggest that change was revolutionary; Ampleforth had long had blessedly good lines of communication between boys and monks, and an inspector visiting the school at the time noticed how much everyone seemed to talk to each other. That had long been the case.

Still, it was disturbing to many when the requirement for Mass daily, twice on Sundays, plus Vespers, was changed. This meant the abandonment of two cherished positions: first, that the grace of the sacrament *ex opere operato*, in the scholastic phrase, was such that even an iota of willingness in its reception would bring Christ's victorious presence to the heart of the believer. The second position, linked to the first, was that compulsory religious practice brought a growth of good habit This view was not so much contradicted as balanced by the Second Vatican Council's teaching, that the very essence of religion consists in those internal, voluntary and free acts by which man sets the whole course of his life towards God. Younger members of the Community, some of whom had observed just how completely some of those who had been pillars of Ampleforth in their day had dropped religious practice at university, were not convinced by the results of Ampleforth's old policy. They had also noticed that the practice by which most of the school went voluntarily to confession on Saturday nights had simply stopped. The Community was prepared to rethink, and did so with energy. A new world of House Mass for groups, of retreats for sixth formers in the monastery, of House Penance Services came into being. The School Retreat was transformed into House-based retreats. This provided, and provides, new opportunities for involvement by the Community in the Catholic practice of the school. When the first lay Housemasters were appointed, the monk priests who became chaplains found new spheres of work, and new relationships with students.

Classes in religious instruction became religious studies, and the department itself was eventually renamed 'Christian Theology', while, at the initiative of Fr Timothy Wright, the entry of boys for public examinations in the subject on a systematic basis became one of the characteristic marks of an Ampleforth education. Undoubtedly, the department remains amongst the most demanding in the school; and, undoubtedly, a continuous effort is needed,

Photographic darkroom, Sunley Centre.

Nevill House, St Dunstan's and St Oswald's, looking east towards the Abbey church.

especially to find ways to relate liturgy and intellectual activity to personal growth in faith and prayer. The enormous task of growing into the Council's vision remains with us. But that in an explicitly Catholic school prayer together and in public should be a part of the day and week, that in a Benedictine school the liturgy and its music should follow best traditional practice – this is a position that can be comfortably defended.

Basketball, Saint Alban Centre.

The 1980s saw Ampleforth's third appeal, carried through by Fr Felix Stephens during Fr Dominic Milroy's headmastership. Fr Dominic had been a Housemaster and had then had some years as Prior of St Anselmo, the Benedictine Abbey which is the seat of the Abbot Primate in Rome. He was very familiar with the thinking of the previous decades, and had contributed to it. Now the Old House was demolished to make way for a new Central Building, which provided accommodation for the Headmaster and secretaries, and moved the Common Room back to the centre, providing new staff workrooms and a main hall so that for the first time the visitor to Ampleforth knew that he had arrived at the centre of the Abbey and College. Fr Dominic consulted about development and was able to push forward with a new music school, adjacent to the gymnasium so that in the course of time the gymnasium might be adapted for orchestral rehearsals, an aim achieved in 2001. Fr Dominic was aware of the growth of interest in design education, and so the Sunley Centre was the final fruit of the third appeal, providing for the first time a fully equipped centre for art, design, photography and technology.

Both Fr Patrick and Fr Dominic had worked with a growing lay teaching staff. Up to 1964, no lay master had been head of any department, other than in an honorary sense as being the teacher of the most able. At that point, John Willcox, the former England rugby captain, arrived as games master, the first layman in such a position. He was to transform the training and the results of the First XV, and, even more important for the sake of Ampleforth's education, to encourage high standards of commitment and sportsmanship. However, there were distinguished lay masters still active as late as the 1980s who had joined Ampleforth's staff on the clear understanding that they were there just to teach, and not to take part in any extracurricular, administrative or pastoral activity. By 1992, when Fr Dominic retired, almost every academic department was headed by a lay master, and John Willcox had been appointed Ampleforth's first lay Housemaster. About this time, the first full-time women teachers arrived on the staff. Pat Boulton became Ampleforth's first special needs teacher. Lucy Warrack and Pam Long joined the English and maths departments under Fr Dominic and by the 1990s women held major responsibilities. Just as the appointment of the first lay masters for academic subjects had been necessary in the late 1920s if Ampleforth was to reach the highest standards, so now with a larger and more complicated school we needed a much more intimate and profound co-operation. This did not diminish the Community's commitment to the school, expressed throughout the period by its support for every significant development, or the willingness of younger monks, most of them not educated at Ampleforth, to commit themselves to this work. By 2000, there were three lay Housemast-ers, and monk priests were working successfully as chaplains in the Houses, a new role which provides a promise of a relationship and service to the young as valuable as any done by their predecessors in the work.

Indoor rifle Range.

Ampleforth's name had become increasingly known among schools in Fr Paul's time, but the last 40 years have brought greater prominence. Abbot Basil Hume had taught theology to the younger brethren for some years, and had taught both History and French in the school, becoming Senior Master (as the heads of department were known until the 1995 inspection suggested a change of title) of Modern Languages and Housemaster of St Bede's. So he carried a special combination of experience when he went to Westminster to become Archbishop in 1976. Just before this, Fr Patrick had become the first Catholic Chairman of the Headmasters' Conference in 1975; Fr Dominic was to be the second Catholic to hold that post in his last year as Headmaster in 1992.

These two appointments marked at least the regard in which other Headmasters held our brethren, but they meant more than this. Ours has been a time of perpetual concern with techniques, with the nuts and bolts of education; there has not been a moment in the last 40 years in which the public examination system was not under question, and in which the organisational structures of schooling have not

Sculpture in the Sunley Centre.

been subject to violent shifts. And, at least since the Bullock report on literacy, *A Language for Life*, over 25 years ago, there has been serious concern about standards in schools. It is all a contrast to the steady support of Ampleforth families for the Community's determination on the development of their school. Both Fr Patrick and Fr Dominic stood for something more in the outside world and that common thread is easily discernible within the very different addresses they gave to the Headmasters' Conference at the end of their year in office. Fr Patrick spoke at the time that a Labour government was bent on destroying the direct-grant schools and forbidding academic selection; he looked for a sensible way forward in the interests of near 100,000 children receiving LEA assistance; he wanted to preserve good schools in the national interest. But above all, and in the talk he gave to the Conference in 1971, he urged 'unfailing and unflinching clarity in the expression of the transcendent basis of human freedom'. Had his words been heeded, English education would be in better shape today.

Fr Dominic spoke after the divorce between independent and maintained sectors was almost complete. Eighteen years of Conservative government had failed to address the possibilities of the voucher scheme, and numerous Secretaries of State had floundered around, largely at the mercy of the technicians of education. The one achievement, the establishment of the grant-maintained schools, was already threatened by the Labour party. The mounds of documentation required in schools, even independent ones, were already growing at a frightening rate. Fr Dominic sought to recall his colleagues to the music of good learning, the delight in learning, the encounter with truth, for to think well is the basis of moral action.

Both Fr Patrick and Fr Dominic spoke out of the long tradition of Christian education, and of ideals on which Ampleforth has been built. But conditions alter all the time, and recent years have seen the effective abandonment of religious education during the GCSE years in some famous schools, and its provision for only a small interested minority in the sixth form. While there are still convinced Christians working in Headmasters' Conference schools, the *mores* and outlook of our contemporaries reflect more and more our dechristianised society. The declining numbers in church suggested that Catholics were affected by these developments. At the same time, boarding-school numbers generally dropped, perhaps for many reasons, but certainly many found in independent day education both a cheaper alternative and one that kept their children at home. Ampleforth had resisted the trend until in 1990 a recession brought unemployment and a loss of confidence to the professional classes, leaving a significant number of boarding-school parents in difficulty. Ampleforth's numbers dropped for the first time since the 19th century. Even for boarding families, access was a priority, and that provided a further difficulty for Ampleforth: people wanted schools near home. On the other hand, it became increasingly apparent that when a family was prepared to travel a long way to the school, as was the case with some 80 per cent of Ampleforth families, their reasons for coming were special, and entirely at one with the Community's reasons for maintaining the school. It is safe to say now that after 100 years of growing closer to the established schools of the Anglican tradition, Ampleforth may again now become more distinct, paradoxically so, as for the first time Ampleforth is sharing its aim of education in faith and virtue with families who have lived in the Anglican tradition.

Facing page: *Lunch with the House.*

120

Girls Hockey Team.

The early 1990s were years of some difficulty. In 1991 Abbot Patrick established a lay Advisory Committee, and the availability of that body, to which the Headmaster reports each term, provided encouragement and a new source of expertise. Economic improvement of itself did not change the position; boarding numbers continued to drop nationally each year into the 21st century. But sharply improved examination results at Ampleforth and steady pastoral care by Housemasters, with tutors now attached to Houses, coupled with good communication by the whole teaching staff, reaffirmed the school's reputation. By this time, monastic and lay staff achieved close co-operation at every level. Resident Assistant Housemasters were being appointed, and among senior staff the College Committee discussed every aspect of school administration, while a further significant step was the appointment of Peter Bryan as a lay financial controller by Fr Felix Stephens when he was Procurator; Peter Bryan succeeded Fr Bede Leach as Procurator in 1999.

Development, academic and physical, could not stand still. The HMC inspection of 1995 reported that there were no weak departments at Ampleforth. The introduction of central dining in the greatly extended Upper Building not only raised the standards of catering and hygiene, but also liberated space in the Houses for prep rooms, as had been envisaged by Arup Associates some 25 years earlier. Some of the spending during this period was, of necessity, defensive, and reflected rising staff costs and dilapidated kitchens around the Houses that would have cost even more to update. But it was always related to the main priority of a better provision for teaching and better accommodation. Investment in the 1990s established a computer network in the school, and enabled Ampleforth to establish a partnership for three years with a Catholic voluntary aided school, St Mary's, Menston. Ampleforth's fourth appeal, headed for two years by Fr Luke Beckett and taken over in 2001 by a newly appointed professional, John Russell, addressed these needs. The Bamford Centre provided completely new and first class facilities for Science and modern studies (Business Studies, Economics, Politics) thanks especially to the generosity of Sir Anthony Bamford. In turn, the redevelopment of the old laboratories as classrooms and a sixth form

Hume House, 2001

common room (named the Matthews Room, after Abbot Edmund Matthews who established Ampleforth's Sixth Form) brought the disappearance of the wooden buildings which had disfigured the heart of the Quadrangle for so long. Hume House was built to accomodate two school Houses, releasing the former St Cuthbert's for use by the monastery and allowing plans to be made for the refurbishment of all the Houses. St Aidan's became the girls' House, retaining its name at their request, and a new building was constructed for it. The objectives of the appeal extended further, to the provision of an all-weather games surface and refurbishment in the theatre, both under way by 2002.

With a new prospectus, a website and video, and professional advice in public relations, by 2001 enquiries and registrations for the school had risen considerably, and entry figures began to rise; at the beginning of the 21st century, Ampleforth's numbers were again above 500. The boarding environment had also changed. With exeats and half term breaks, families no longer felt cut off from their children for months at a time. Also with improved communications, including a rapid and fairly reliable train service from London, travel to Ampleforth from other parts of the country had become much less daunting. Even Ampleforth's (albeit diminished) isolation began to find a renewed appeal, as the problems of the city environment became a matter of growing concern for parents.

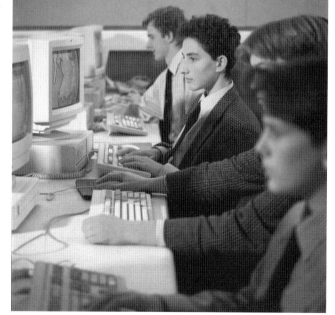

The rise in numbers was faster because some of the new entry were girls. In fact, Ampleforth's first girl, now Dr Fiona Forsythe, the daughter of the fondly remembered chemistry teacher, left in 1973. Fr Patrick had made this provision for daughters of lay staff, and Fr Dominic accepted some others. The position was regularised in 1999, when the school was formally opened to sixth form day girls, and sixth form boarders followed in 2001, when the first Housemistress, Penelope Dixon, was appointed. There had been a growing pattern of requests from parents, and although some had an understandable concern

123

about the implications of such a modification of Ampleforth's traditional education, there was also evidence of strong support for the development. The change in the style of university education had implications for the sixth form of a boarding school. Further, for some years there had been no Catholic boarding school for girls in the north of England. Under Abbot Timothy's guidance, the Community again supported a radical step, but one intended to allow Ampleforth to provide for its families what was needed. In a pleasing revival of 19th century terminology, Ampleforth's boys and girls became 'students'.

In an institution so dependent on public confidence, and therefore sensitive to current needs, adapting and changing to meet them, it is tempting to recall the story of the handle and the axe: it was a good axe, said the workman – it had only had four new handles and one new head in 40 years. While the principle of development assures the continuity and identity of the Church, no institution within the Church has that guarantee. Yet while the Mission Statement, a typically 1990s tool for the setting down of what has always been hitherto assumed, would not have been written in that form in an earlier time, it may be that an earlier generation would have recognised it. Similarly, we can recognise much of our current practice in Fr Paul Nevill's seminal article in the *Ampleforth Journal* of 1912, 'Liberty and Responsibility for Boys'. Fr Dominic reminded his fellow heads in 1991 that obedience is the way to liberty; through obedience to the discipline of learning, we achieve the freedom of the wise. In offering our students liberty, we invite them to accept for them-

124

selves the discipline they need. In offering them still some responsibility for others, a real share in the government of the school, we invite them to care for others, and especially for the young. It is true that failures do happen – as has always been the case. Perhaps more importantly, it helps also to recall Fr Paul's detailed school rules of 1927, with items which today would be left within the province of the Housemaster. Historians are always aware of the way in which context changes perception. The liberty of which Fr Paul wrote was a liberty within safer bounds than exist now; and the responsibility was a responsibility in a world better ordered than it is now.

The question is still whether what Ampleforth does for its students is something that must be preserved. After a lifetime in independent education at the end of a century in which Ampleforth's work has been so painfully built up, a monk and priest must be aware that an activity regarded as praiseworthy and moral down the centuries has become regarded by some as socially divisive and harmful. Moreover, governments of both parties have now much enlarged the state's powers over our schools, by way of inspection and regulation. Leaving aside arguments that might apply to any independent school – that, for example, government should not have control of every aspect of national and cultural life – what is it that justifies the devotion this Community has given for so long? It must be, first, that what is given by way of invitation to learn of the Christian life is beyond class and beyond the claims of secular society. We would do it without charge if we could, but we do not have the means. Secondly, in spite of all human failings, Ampleforth strives after excellence in every respect, successfully, as the inspection report of 2002 affirmed. Finally, the justification must lie in the lives of those who pass through this place. It does not matter in principle whether they become well-known or even whether they are successful; what matters is how they live within the circle of their family, their work and their acquaintances. The evidence for this must always be anecdotal, but it is sometimes heartwarming.

14

Ampleforth Alumni by Sir David Goodhall

For the first hundred years of its existence, Ampleforth was a small school, remote even by the standards of the day. In its very early years, despite its remoteness, and owing largely to the vigorous and imaginative leadership of Fr Augustine Baines, it had prospered and attracted a number of boys from aristocratic families. But following the break-up in 1830, most of these families looked elsewhere for the education of their sons, and Ampleforth's standing relative to other Catholic schools and colleges declined. For the rest of the century it relied heavily on its strong links with Lancashire and the north, dating back to the Community's time at Dieulouard, developing a particularly strong (and inter-related) constituency in and around Liverpool.

Moreover for much of the 19th century about half the boys in the school were 'church students', i.e. intended for the priesthood; so the great majority of notable old boys in this period were priests, and most of them Benedictines. Bishop Baines himself; Fr Wilfrid Cooper, the Prior who built the old Abbey Church; Fr Lawrence Shepherd, who sowed the first seeds of the monastic revival among the English Benedictines; Fr Anselm Burge, the Prior who brought Ampleforth into the mainstream of British intellectual life by opening the house at Oxford which became St Benet's Hall; and Bishop Hedley, after Manning probably the greatest and certainly the most learned of the 19th-century English Catholic Bishops; these (like many other eminent sons of Ampleforth down to the present day) were all of them monks.

Old boy priests who were not monks of Ampleforth included Fr Peter Hutton, the first president of Ratcliffe, and Dom Wilfrid Alcock, founding Superior of St Augustine's Abbey, Ramsgate.

The typical 19th-century Amplefordian came from a relatively modest, middle class family, probably in the north of England. Often he would have relations among the monks. The hierarchy's ban on Catholics going to Oxford and Cambridge, not finally lifted (through the exertions of Bishop Hedley) until 1895, barred him from most of the higher reaches of national life. So if he did not become a priest, he would follow in his father's footsteps to become a doctor, a lawyer, a merchant or the proprietor of a family business. Doctors were particularly numerous. A few became land agents, and many were local magistrates. Joseph Holdforth

The RAF meets Fr Paul, centre, 1945: Michael Maxwell, left, Roderick Chisholm, right.

(arrived 1825), a silk merchant, became Mayor of Leeds and received Cardinal Wiseman on his visit there. James Gibson Dees (1862), a JP and County Councillor for Cumberland, was Lord Lonsdale's Agent at Whitehaven.

Such men were strong traditional Catholics, active in good works in their local communities and deeply loyal to Ampleforth, but with no pretensions to national distinction. Bishop Hedley himself was of this background, being the son of a doctor, the brother of another and the cousin of a third. The Goodall family doctor, John Pegge Gornall (1875), was the son and grandson of doctors from the Fylde, both of whom had been at Ampleforth in its heroic age.

One old boy, singled out for special honours at the Ampleforth Dinner at Liverpool in 1900 on his election as Mayor of Barrow-in-Furness, can be taken as a typically successful Amplefordian of his generation. John Peter Smith, son of a Lancaster merchant, came to Ampleforth in 1875, trained as an engineer and became a prosperous corn miller. In 1891, at the early age of 27, he became a Barrow Councillor and a J.P., and was Mayor of the town during two Coronation years (1901–02 and 1911–12). He was President of the Barrow Chamber of Commerce and the Barrow Cricket Club, and a pillar of the Catholic Records Society. When his son Basil, also an Amplefordian, was killed in the First World War, he founded a Leaving Scholarship at Ampleforth in his memory; and according to his obituary in the *Ampleforth Journal*, a 'fine Catholic spirit . . . animated all that he undertook'.

John William Polidori.

It would be misleading, however, to think that all 19th-century Amplefordians were solid north countrymen. Of the 1,634 boys known to have been at Ampleforth between 1802 and 1895, 81 (nearly 5 per cent) came from Ireland and a further 123 from overseas, some from as far afield as India, Australia, Canada and Latin America. Robert Nihell came to the school from Antigua in 1815, and James Dowling from Calcutta in 1822. James Leigh (1840), who came from London, is recorded as being 'a convert from Buddhism'. Thirty-one boys came from France, mainly from Lille, where there seems to have been a regular nest of Amplefordians in the 1850s and 60s. Alexandre Pécoul (1895), from Paris, Captain of the School in 1899, whose family had a large estate in Martinique, went into French politics and was studying the French colonies with a view to becoming a colonial Deputy in the National Assembly when he was shipwrecked and drowned at the Rapids of Se Bang in Indo-China in 1904.

Prominent among the early exotics was John William Polidori, who arrived in 1806, the eldest son of a distinguished Italian scholar who had been secretary to Alfieri and had translated Milton into Italian. On leaving Ampleforth, Polidori qualified as a doctor at Edinburgh and became personal physician and travelling companion to Lord Byron, who often mentions him (affectionately but a shade contemptuously) in his journals as 'Polly-Dolly'. Through Byron, Polidori came to know Shelley (whom he at one point improbably challenged to a duel) and Shelley's wife Mary, the author of Frankenstein. At about the same time, he was prompted to write a Gothic novel of his own (*Ernestus Berchthold*, suggestively subtitled *The Modern Oedipus*) and a novella, *The Vampyre*. The latter, being falsely attributed by the publishers to Byron and praised by Goethe, achieved considerable notoriety and is regarded as the parent of all subsequent vampire stories, culminating in Bram Stoker's Dracula.

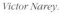

Victor Narey.

After leaving Byron's service, Polidori became romantically involved with Elizabeth and Harriet Martineau, and followed up this unsuccessful affaire by proposing himself to join the novitiate at Ampleforth – a proposal understandably, if somewhat sanctimoniously, declined by the Prior, Fr Lawrence Burgess. He then attempted to study for the Bar, but soon fell

Joseph Pike at Ampleforth, 1892, inset, and during the First World War.

victim to depression, dying – probably by his own hand – in 1825. His portrait in the National Portrait Gallery is by Gainsford, Ampleforth's first Art Master.

No other early Amplefordian can compete with Polidori in terms either of notoriety or (as far as is known) of eccentricity. But another name which catches the eye in the early lists is that of 'Prince Iturbite' (sic), shown as coming to Ampleforth in 1826 from Mexico. To this name is appended the intriguing note: 'Son of the Emperor of Mexico. Came to Ampleforth as a Parlour Boarder. Later, Mexican Ambassador to the English Court. Shot during a revolution.' Mexico achieved its independence from Spain in 1821 under General Agustin de Iturbide, who then proclaimed himself Emperor. In 1823, having been forced to abdicate, he visited England, and in 1824 unwisely returned to Mexico, where he was summarily shot. How the son came to Ampleforth two years after his father's death, went on to become an ambassador and was then himself shot, remains mysterious. Even in a decade when the small school contained three future peers (Arundell of Wardour, Clifford of Chudleigh and Stafford), a Mexican Prince must have been an interesting and unusual figure.

Parlour boarders recur at Ampleforth during the 19th century. They appear to have been young men of university age, who, debarred from Oxford or Cambridge, could presumably expect to receive some tuition (and supervision) from the monks. Archbishop Ullathorne, who taught briefly at Ampleforth in the 1830s, records in his *Cabin Boy to Archbishop* how he dealt with 'insubordination by a young man, son of a baronet, living among the religious'. Later examples include Austin Ferrers Bateman (1857) who became a benefactor of the house and built the Catholic church in Helmsley, and Prince Krasicyn Sapieha from Poland, who came to Ampleforth in 1890 to learn English.

It would be interesting also to know more about Felix McCarthy, who came to the school in 1829 from London, described in a note as a cousin of Cardinal Wiseman and 'endowed with an extraordinary memory. Whole books of Virgil were at his command . . . was knighted later. Married the daughter of a Governor of Ceylon'. He was perhaps confused with Charles James McCarthy, knighted in 1857 as Colonial Secretary in Ceylon, but not in the Ampleforth lists.

Nor was Ampleforth entirely deserted by the Catholic nobility and squirearchy after 1830 (although most of those who came were younger sons). Successive generations of Stourtons, for example, figure in the school lists down to the present day; and when Bishop Baines's smarter connections transferred their allegiance to Prior Park, Sir Thomas Massey-Stanley of Hooton insisted on his two sons remaining at Ampleforth, as did Mr Blundell of Crosby. The elder Blundell, Nicholas, went on to be a Deputy Lieutenant for Lancashire, commanded the Duke of Lancaster's Own Rifle Militia and became a talented artist, decorating St Mary's Church, Crosby, with his own hands and beautifying that at Blundellsands, of which he was co-founder. His brother William, a lieutenant in the 51st Regiment (later the King's Own Yorkshire Light Infantry, the KOYLI), was killed in action at Rangoon in 1852.

William Blundell's choice of career was untypical. Although in the 20th century the school was to develop strong links with the Army, in the 19th century relatively few Amplefordians became soldiers. Prior to Catholic Emancipation in 1829, Catholics had been debarred from holding commissions in the Armed Forces, so the Catholic middle class had no military tradition behind it; and the Army would in any case have been beyond the means of many Ampleforth families in the days when it was hardly possible for a junior officer to live on his pay, and promotion was by purchase. If any old boys enlisted in the ranks, their names have not been recorded; and the few who took commissions seem predictably to have come from the wealthier, well-connected families.

For example, George Waterton (1816), a cousin of Squire Waterton the naturalist, became a Captain of Hussars 'in the Austrian Service'; John Stanley (1830), the elder of the two sons of Sir Thomas Massey-Stanley mentioned above, who married a Talleyrand and inherited his father's baronetcy, became a Captain in the 60th Rifles; Thomas Mostyn of Talacre (1827) became a Captain in the 54th Regiment; and Francis Salvin (1833), the son of William Salvin of Croxdale Park, Co Durham, was a Captain in the York and Lancaster Regiment. Everard Stourton (1842), a Captain in the 8th Hussars, served in both the Crimea and the Indian Mutiny; while Lieutenant Thomas Chisholm (1852) died in the Mutiny of cholera during a forced march 'after fighting six battles'. John Jerningham (1830), a younger son of Lord Stafford, fell overboard from his troopship and was drowned while on the way to India in 1838. Naval connections seem even fewer: only Bernard Cooper of Brough Hall (1845), who died in Rome, is recorded as having been 'a Captain in the Royal Navy.'

Herbert Railton ARIBA.

Both music and drawing flourished at Ampleforth in the later years of the 19th century under long-serving 'professors'. Concerts and operatic performances marked most major festive occasions, including the Exhibition weekends. From this musical tradition came William Marsh (1892), who composed the State song of Texas ('Texas, Our Texas'), and some distinguished monk-amateurs: Fr Egbert Turner (1862), who died in 1897, was a well-known composer of Masses for church choirs; later on Fr Bernard McElligott (1907) was a nationally regarded exponent of Plainsong, founding the Society of St Gregory in 1929; while Fr Laurence Bevenot (1919) was another successful composer of liturgical music. But it was in the field of art and architecture that lay Amplefordians made their mark.

Of these, the most celebrated (although his fame came late) was Roderic O'Conor, the Irish impressionist, who came to the school from Ireland (where his father was High Sheriff of Roscommon) in 1873. He became a friend of Gauguin, lived most of his life in Paris (exhibiting at the Paris Salon and the Salon des Indépendants), and died in France in 1940. Like everyone who studied art at Ampleforth at that time, he would have been taught by William Boddy of York, the art master from 1858 until 1908. Boddy was a skilled professional watercolourist, but he had trained as an architect, and seems to have been particularly successful in imbuing his pupils with a love of drawing. A glance through the early numbers of the *Journal* or Fr Cuthbert Almond's *History of Ampleforth Abbey* (published in 1903 to mark the first centenary) reveals a profusion of remarkably accomplished line drawings by amateurs and professionals alike, all of them Boddy's pupils, notable among them being Fr Maurus Powell (1887), and the future architect Alfred Rigby (1894).

Outstanding among the professionals was Herbert Railton ARIBA (1872), one of the few Amplefordians to be found in the *Dictionary of National Biography*, who supplied the frontispiece for Fr Cuthbert's History. The original of that drawing – 'Ampleforth Abbey from the South West' – now hangs in the cloister and amply bears out all that has been said about Railton's delicacy of line and tone. Railton, who came to the school in 1882 from Blackburn, had (like Boddy) trained as an architect, but gave up architecture for drawing. He is credited with having started a widely imitated school of illustration, among his followers being Joseph Pike (1892), whose pencil sketches appeared frequently in the *Illustrated London News* and the *Sphere*. Pike also exhibited at the Royal Academy and published a sketchbook of evocative drawings of Ampleforth as it was in 1920.

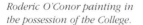

Roderic O'Conor painting in the possession of the College.

Among a succession of late Victorian Amplefordian architects, probably the most gifted was Joseph Stanislaus Hansom (1862), whose father (inventor of the Hansom cab) and uncle between them designed the old Abbey Church. After leaving school, the younger Hansom

Bernard Burge (1919).

Francis de Guingand.

volunteered as a Zouave in the papal Army, then still fighting in defence of the Papal States, and was decorated by Pope Pius IX. He then took up his father's profession, became a FRIBA and designed a number of important Catholic churches. Of these, St Walburga at Preston, the Holy Name at Manchester and St Philip Neri at Arundel (now the Cathedral) are described by the architectural historian, Professor James Stevens Curl as being 'of particular distinction'. Also well known are St Aloysius at Oxford and the Servite Church at Fulham. Hansom founded the Catholic Record Society; and was for a time the Hon. Secretary of the Ampleforth Society, started in 1875 'to unite old boys and friends of St Lawrence's in furthering the interests of the College'. Its first President was George Chamberlain JP of Birkdale (1838), great-grandfather of the present Headmaster.

Hansom was, however, unsuccessful in the competition to design the New Monastery in 1892, which was limited to 'past pupils and those who have done work for the College previously'. Five Amplefordian architects, including Hansom, submitted designs, the winner being Bernard Smith (1860) from Bungay, a sensitive and retiring figure who had worked for a time as an architectural engineer in Gibraltar and travelled extensively (on a Royal Academy scholarship) in Spain, Germany and France, the influence of French Gothic being clearly discernible in his work at Ampleforth.

Shortly after the New Monastery was completed, the Boer War broke out. A number of old boys fought in South Africa, either as regular officers or as volunteers, and two of the monks – Fr Denis Firth (1865) and Fr Stephen Dawes (1886) (another doctor's son) – served as Army Chaplains. More old boys now began to join the Army as regulars, and the informal cadet force became a properly constituted OTC in 1911. In 1909, extensive manoeuvres were held on the Hambleton Hills under the stern eye of General Sir John French, in which the Yorkshire Mounted Brigade, a local Yeomanry unit, was commanded by Captain Sir William Austin (1883), later Master of the East Galway Foxhounds.

From the earliest days of the school, Amplefordians were to be found in every quarter of the globe. The annotated school lists, the early numbers of the *Journal*, and its predecessor the *Ampleforth Diary*, record old boys in Australia, Canada, Nova Scotia, New Zealand and Siam. Joseph Moore (1846) had become 'editor of a newspaper in Sydney'; Thomas Fairhurst (1856) 'a tea merchant in China' and Neil Fox (1857) a civil engineer in India. Marmaduke Manley (1885), Ernest Primavesi (1886) and John Carroll (1886) were drawn to the Klondyke in the Gold Rush of 1898. Observing that two of the three were 'tenderfeet', the *Journal* commented: 'It is a stern school they are entered in. We hope the process of hardening will confine itself to the extremities.'

The first recorded Amplefordian Judge, Edgar Meynell (1837), a former Recorder of Doncaster and a Judge of the Durham County Court, died in 1901; and in 1905 occurs the first mention of an old boy in the Colonial Service: George Nevill (1889), shortly to become British Resident at Sokoto in Nigeria. He was followed later by Cuthbert Mayne CMG (1917), who spent his whole career in Nigeria, becoming Senior Resident at Calabar and Deputy Governor of Eastern Nigeria. 'He won and retained, at a time of almost revolutionary change, the genuine and deep affection not only of his British colleagues . . . but also of countless Nigerians, politicians, business men and simple peasant farmers alike.' On the other side of the world, Edward Emerson (1907) – Sir Edward Emerson KC as he was to become – was making a distinguished career in Newfoundland, where he became Minister of Justice, Attorney-General and finally, in 1944, Chief Justice of the Supreme Court.

Ampleforth's development into a major public school had begun to gather momentum with the appointment of Fr Edmund Matthews as Headmaster in 1903; and the First World War can be said to mark the school's entrance on to the national stage. By 1914, there were still only about 120 boys in the school; yet in the following four years 375 old boys served in the Armed Forces, of whom no less than 64 were killed in action and at least eleven won the MC. The great majority were junior officers, almost all of them commemorated by moving obituaries in the *Journal*, often accompanied by photographs. The most senior among those who served was the Hon. Edward Stourton (later Corbally-Stourton) (1893). Already decorated for bravery as a subaltern in South Africa, he was appointed to the staff after being twice wounded, was mentioned in despatches four times and awarded the DSO, and went on after the War to command the 1st Battalion of his own regiment, the KOYLI.

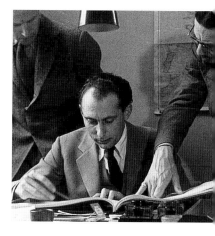

Harman Grisewood, seated.

The First World War also marks Ampleforth's first appearance (so far as is known) in fiction. In Bruce Marshal's *All Glorious Within* there occurs the not unsympathetic figure of the drinking Major, who 'had been educated at Ampleforth, but since then racketed about a lot.'

The years between the two World Wars were a time of rapid expansion, when, in the words of Archbishop Mathew, 'the abbey church . . . Gilling and the Gilbert Scott school houses became factors in the general English social landscape' – a landscape in which Amplefordians also began to figure more prominently, and in greater numbers. In 1930 John Somers Cocks (1925), later Consul-General at Munich, became the first to join the Diplomatic Service, starting a trend which increased significantly after the Second World War. In the Indian Civil Service – 'the Heaven born' – Bernard Burge (1919), a nephew of Abbot Anselm Burge, served as Deputy Magistrate of Midnapore in Bengal, and was assassinated there in 1933. He is commemorated (in exemplary Latin) by a tablet in the Abbey Church, and a memorial bust was erected at Midnapore itself 'subscribed almost entirely by his Indian friends and admirers'. Unveiling it, his Divisional Commissioner, in a tone nicely redolent of the period, observed that 'With Europeans he was hail-fellow-well-met. With Indians he was invariably courteous and considerate.' It would be interesting to know if the bust is still there.

Francis De Guingand (1918), afterwards Major-General Sir Francis, KBE CB DSO, Chief of Staff to Field-Marshal Montgomery and pall-bearer at his funeral, was in the school during the First World War, as was René Hague (1922), the printer and designer, disciple and son-in-law of Eric Gill and lifelong friend of David Jones, whose portrait drawing of Hague is in the Leeds City Art Gallery. Other distinguished men who followed them included Edward Turville-Petre FBA (1926), Professor of Icelandic Literature at Oxford from 1953 to 1975; Harman Grisewood CBE (1924), a key figure in the BBC, first as creator of the Third Programme and later as Director of the Spoken Word and assistant to the Director-General; Lord Lovat (1929), who was to win the DSO and the MC and briefly hold junior Ministerial Office in 1945; his brother Hugh (Hon Sir Hugh Fraser MBE MP) (1935), the first Amplefordian to attain a seat in the Cabinet (as Secretary of State for Air from 1962 to 1964), and incidentally co-founder of the the *Ampleforth News*; and Patrick O'Donovan (1937), for nearly thirty years chief foreign correspondent of *The Observer*.

Patrick O'Donovan at school.

Of this inter-War generation, it was Harman Grisewood who best evoked the special quality of an Ampleforth education in the tribute he paid to it shortly before his death:

'We were taught by men whose Benedictine Catholic devotion was made evident to us. These men shared our lives – at meal times and on the playing fields, at morning prayers

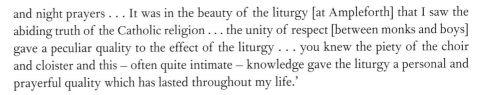

and night prayers . . . It was in the beauty of the liturgy [at Ampleforth] that I saw the abiding truth of the Catholic religion . . . the unity of respect [between monks and boys] gave a peculiar quality to the effect of the liturgy . . . you knew the piety of the choir and cloister and this – often quite intimate – knowledge gave the liturgy a personal and prayerful quality which has lasted throughout my life.'

Michael Allmand VC.

Hugh Dormer MC.

An SAS jeep patrol met on its return from the desert by its commander, Colonel David Stirling, right, during the 1940–43 campaign in North African.

The Second World War affected Ampleforth as profoundly as the First. Once again, every number of the *Journal* became filled with the obituaries of old boys killed in action, with extracts from letters from the front and citations for gallantry. From the larger school (378 boys in 1939) over a thousand served in the Armed Forces, 132 in the Royal Navy, 693 in the Army and 193 in the Royal Air Force. 121 lost their lives. One old boy, Michael Allmand (1941), won a posthumous VC; there were some 20 DSOs, 10 DSCs, 35 MCs and 26 DFCs. Three of the monks served as chaplains, Fr George Forbes (1920) (who had been a subaltern in the Grenadier Guards before entering the Monastery) winning the MC.

As with the First War, no one could attempt to chronicle all the suffering or all the acts of courage and self sacrifice which these figures reflect. Every name deserves to be remembered. Only a few examples may be given here. Captain Michael Allmand had read History at Oriel; and his interests were literary and artistic rather than military: he had helped to found the *Wind and the Rain* and had written a life of Edmund Burke. In a letter from the front foretelling his own death, he wrote that to die for his country and 'for peace and happiness for others in this troubled world . . . is really a great privilege, and though I would have given anything to have died instead for Christ and the Catholic Church, I think that this way is a good second best.' He won his posthumous VC in Burma, for 'superb gallantry, outstanding leadership and protracted heroism.'

Another soldier whose 'interests were those of the mind' was Lieutenant Michael Fenwick (1938), Royal Scots, a scholar of Lincoln College, Oxford and a writer of religious verse of distinction, who 'little though he knew it, was an adornment to his home, to his school and wherever his influence came to bear.' He had been hoping to try his vocation at Ampleforth after the war; but he was killed, aged 21, in the unsuccessful defence of Hong Kong. Captain Hugh Dormer (1937), Irish Guards, killed in Normandy in 1944, was awarded the DSO for hazardous secret operations in enemy-occupied France, his account of those operations, published as *Hugh Dormer's Diaries*, being one of the minor classics to come out of the War. The words with which the Diaries end deserve to be quoted, because they encapsulate a Christian sensibility of which Ampleforth could be proud:

I face the adventure [returning to the front line, where he was killed] in sober determination . . . knowing that modern armoured war is Hell, and complete Hell, and nothing else, with no nobility or fineness about it, but only humiliating fear. Once again at Mass this morning in the village church I offered my life to God to do with it entirely as He chooses. Should He take it, then indeed would I go forth eagerly to meet death, having only the sorrow for my mother left behind. But then all men must die some time, and for a long time I have felt a stranger on this earth. *Cio che Dio vuole io voglio.*

The Amplefordian best known to the public in connection with the War was probably David Stirling (1934) – Colonel Sir David Stirling DSO KT – founder of the Special Air Service (SAS), of whom Field Marshal Lord Bramall wrote on his death in 1990 that he had built up the SAS 'through his strong and abiding faith . . . and through his strength of character which enabled him to persuade others that the impossible was possible . . . The British Army and the nation as a whole has every reason to be proud of this great Amplefordian.' A generation later, Captain Robert Nairac, Grenadier Guards (1966), who won a posthumous GC for undercover operations in Northern Ireland during which he was murdered by the IRA in 1977, was in the same tradition.

In the years which have elapsed since the Second World War ended, old boys of Ampleforth have risen to eminence in almost every sphere of national life: in the arts, in journalism, on the stage and in sport, as well as in scholarship and the universities, in the Armed Forces, in diplomacy and the public service, on the judicial bench and in industry and business. Of the many who are still alive, it would be invidious to mention some at the expense of others. Of the recently dead, a name which must stand out is that of George Basil Hume (1941), Abbot, Archbishop, Cardinal, O.M., one of the great spiritual leaders of his day; and alongside his example it seems appropriate to set that of Philip Lawrence (1965), who left a successful career in independent education to teach in inner-city comprehensives, and won national admiration in 1995 when he fell victim to the culture of violence which he had dedicated his life to overcoming.

Philip Lawrence.

Of recent old boys, the living as well as the dead, some (perhaps rather more than in the past) have distanced themselves from the values which Ampleforth has sought to instil; many others have (often unconsciously) exemplified them. But looking through the obituaries in the *Ampleforth Journal*, one cannot help being struck by the extent to which the pattern set in the 19th century lived on in the much larger and more sophisticated Ampleforth of the 20th.

Catholicism, often (but not always) of a very traditional kind, is deeply engrained. A comment by a son (not an old boy) writing about his father in 1985 could be echoed in many other cases: 'Dad was always grateful and indebted to the example given by, and the faith handed on by, the Fathers of Ampleforth . . . I do want you to know that here was one Old Boy who valued beyond words what you gave him and impressed it on me.' Community service of one sort and another features frequently. The spectrum of occupations and ways of making a living has greatly widened, the social background is less provincial and the level of professional or other achievement higher than a hundred years earlier. But the average Amplefordian still seems content to make relatively little noise in the world and to be modestly rather than spectacularly successful, as the world judges success.

St Benedict, by Judy Brown.

It is for others to judge how far this is due to lack of ambition (or ruthlessness), and how far it results from a Benedictine distaste for careerism and self-promotion which is inherently admirable; from an awareness, conscious or otherwise, of the tension implicit in an Ampleforth education between the aspiration to professional and social success on the one hand and the demands of the Christian life on the other. It is perhaps enough if it can be said of Ampleforth old boys, as George Eliot said of Dorothea at the end of *Middlemarch*, that 'the effect of her being upon those around her was incalculably diffusive: for the growing good of the world is partly dependent on unhistoric acts; and that things are not so ill with you and me as they might have been, is half owing to the number who live faithfully a hidden life, and rest in unvisited tombs.' It is a thought of which St Benedict, I think, would approve.

PICTURE ACKNOWLEDGEMENTS

B. Scotson (O62) 3; Fr Gordon Beattie (B59) 15, 32, 39, 65, 88;
Bodleian Library, Oxford 11; Royal Commission on Historical Monuments 19, 38;
Stephen Hyde (B77) & Mark Pickthall (B76) 26, 37, 56, 57, 58, 75, 77, 85, 87, 101, 105, 113–125 passim;
St Benet's Hall 41, 45; Michael Dunne (A46) 50; Fairfax House, York 68; G. Wood 69; St Louis Abbey 81;
National Portrait Gallery 130; Hulton Getty 131; The Art Archive 132 (bottom); PA Photos 133 (top).

All other images are from Ampleforth Abbey Archives.